melinda barta

# custom
## cool
## jewelry

**INTERWEAVE**
INTERWEAVEBOOKS.COM

**PHOTOGRAPHY** Joe Coca
**PHOTO STYLING** Kevin Hardiek
**COVER & INTERIOR DESIGN** Pamela Norman
**ILLUSTRATIONS** Gayle Ford, Ann Swanson,
Dustin Wedekind
**EDITOR** Katrina Loving
**TECHNICAL EDITOR** Jamie Hogsett

INTERWEAVEBOOKS.COM
Interweave Press LLC
201 East Fourth Street
Loveland, CO 80537-5655 USA
interweavebooks.com

Printed in China by Asia Pacific Offset

Library of Congress
Cataloging-in-Publication Data
Barta, Melinda A.
  Custom cool jewelry : create 200+ personalized
pendants, charms, and clasps / Melinda Barta,
author.
      p. cm.
  Includes index.
  ISBN 978-1-59668-074-6 (pbk.)
  1. Jewelry making. 2. Wire craft.
  3. Beadwork. I. Title.
  TT212.B37285 2008
  739.27--dc22
                  2008003845

10 9 8 7 6 5 4 3 2 1

# acknowledgments

IT PROBABLY GOES without saying that writing a book is a large endeavor and cannot be completed without encouragement and love from close friends and family. A special thank you to Alisa Hjermstad for helping with project samples, her loyal friendship, and for encouraging me to further expand my use of materials. I am grateful for my wonderful immediate and extended family for their undying support—especially my husband, Jason, and mother, Jean, who kept me motivated and focused up to the very last bead strung and word written. Another thanks to Jason for being my chauffeur into the mountains, allowing me to bead on our skiing, camping, and canoeing adventures. I thank my mentor Renie Breskin Adams for her wit, love of craft, and many years of friendship and Danielle Fox for her humor and eye for good design.

Special thanks to the books department of Interweave for turning a proposal that started out as a small box of bead samples into a beautiful book; this includes editorial director Tricia Waddell, managing editor Rebecca Campbell, editor Katrina Loving, technical editor Jamie Hogsett, art director Pamela Norman, photo stylist Kevin Hardiek, illustrator Ann Swanson, and photographer Joe Coca

Thanks to the management team at Interweave, including Linda Ligon, Marlene Blessing, and Marilyn Murphy for giving me an outlet for my creativity and to everyone else at Interweave who helped this book reach your hands. Thank you also to each student I have taught; your love of detail and never-ending desire to learn remind me of why all we beaders and stitchers do what we do.

— **Melinda Barta**

## Special Techniques

# contents

**Introduction 06**

# introduction

FOR ME, MAKING JEWELRY is not just about beads, it is about the process it takes to get to a finished design. Whether finding cool jewelry elements while combing the aisles of bead, fabric, and antique shops, hiking in the woods, or on a city walk with a friend, inspiration for jewelry design doesn't always come from a catalog or bead—it comes to us in many shapes and forms when we least expect it. Inspired, personalized jewelry does more than adorn; it can tell stories, garner compliments, and even commemorate bygone times (such as a necklace made of your grandmother's favorite brooch). The beauty of creating jewelry is that it is all about you and the adventure of self-expression.

The inspiration for this book developed from a desire to create jewelry using more than the traditional jewelry-making techniques and the frustration of not being able to find unique, personalized, and affordable components that perfectly complemented my designs. So I started experimenting with small samples that focused just on the three basic elements of jewelry design— pendants, charms, and clasps. Over 275 samples later, this book was born.

If you love adding a personal touch to jewelry and have a desire for everything you craft to be one-of-a-kind, get ready to start expanding your boundaries. You'll have fun etching glass beads, embossing gift tags, stitching fabric pendants, baking wearable collages with resin, and stamping polymer clay pendants. Plus, incorporating hand-made components ensures that your jewelry will be 100 percent unique, 100 percent yours.

This book is divided into four sections: pendants, charms, clasps, and finished projects. You'll notice that each chapter is chock-full of project variations, so you'll be sure to find something that fits your style. For added inspiration, six full-length projects clearly show you on how to make use of your handmade components in necklaces and bracelets.

If you are new to the basics, or could use a refresher and love insider tips, be sure to check out Beading and Wireworking 101 on p. 130. So get out your tools, hammers, stickers, scissors, glue, needles, threads, fabric—just about anything in your craft stash—and begin taking your jewelry to the next level by adding a personal touch to each and every element. And most importantly—have fun!

**pendant**
/pen—dənt/
*n.* Something
suspended from
something else,
esp. an ornament
or a piece of
jewelry attached
to a necklace
or bracelet.

# pendants

*Do pendants really have more fun?* They must be, they always get all the attention. When you wear an interesting necklace, the focal piece is undoubtedly the first thing to garner comments. In addition to being so much fun to make, the pendants in the following pages will add a unique touch to any of your designs. You will learn to emboss antique playing cards, roll up some polymer clay, stamp and stitch fabric focal pieces, and wire-wrap to your heart's content. From flirty and romantic wireworked dangles to simple and understated polymer clay beads, you'll wear your jewelry with pride—be ready for the compliments!

crystal cascade

lovely links

shimmer
& shell

bejeweled
bubble

# nouveau riche rings

**TOOLBOX**
Wire cutters
Chain-nose pliers
Flat-nose pliers
Round-nose pliers

Warm golds, flirty chains, classic stones, sparkling crystals—with just a few wireworking skills and ingredients like these, you can make an ordinary necklace glamorous. These eye-catching pendants are true conversation pieces, you'll be sure to get the question "Where did you get that?"

## bejeweled bubble

### MATERIALS

6 antique rose 4mm fire-polished rounds

3 labradorite 6x9mm faceted briolettes

2 amazonite 8x10mm faceted teardrops

1 lemon quartz 10x14mm faceted briolette

1 sterling silver 32mm bead hoop

3 gunmetal 1" (25mm) head pins

3 sterling silver 1" (25mm) head pins

1 gunmetal 5mm jump ring

2" (5 cm) of sterling silver 2mm round chain

3" (7.5 cm) of gunmetal 2x4mm twisted oval chain

12" (30.5 cm) of sterling silver 24-gauge wire

1~**DANGLES.** Make 6 dangles:

**Dangle 1:** Use a gunmetal head pin to string 1 fire-polished round and form a simple loop that attaches to the end of a $7/8$" (2.2 cm) piece of gunmetal chain.

Repeat twice, attaching simple-loop dangles to other links of the same chain.

**Dangle 2:** Use 2" (5 cm) of sterling silver wire to string 1 amazonite teardrop; form a wrapped-loop bail that attaches to the end of a $3/8$" (1 cm) piece of sterling silver chain.

Repeat using a labradorite briolette that attaches to the other end of the chain (when later stringing this dangle, pass through the top of this bail).

**Dangle 3:** Use 2" (5 cm) of sterling silver wire to string 1 amazonite teardrop; form a wrapped-loop bail that attaches to the end of a ¾" (2 cm) piece of gunmetal chain.

**Dangle 4:** Use 2" (5 cm) of sterling silver wire to string 1 lemon quartz briolette; form a wrapped-loop bail that attaches to the end of a $3/8$" (1 cm) piece of sterling silver chain.

**Dangle 5:** Use 2" (5 cm) of sterling silver wire to string 1 labradorite briolette; form a wrapped-loop bail that attaches to the end of a 1⅛" (3 cm) piece of gunmetal chain.

Repeat to attach an additional labradorite briolette to another link of the same chain.

**Dangle 6:** Use a sterling silver head pin to string 1 fire-polished round and form a wrapped loop that attaches to the end of a 1" (2.5 cm) piece of sterling silver chain.

Repeat to attach 2 additional fire-polished rounds to the same chain.

**2~ HOOP.** Create a small simple loop on each end of the hoop; the loops should not point up; instead, when the loop is laid flat on the work surface, the loops will blend in with the continuous shape of the circle.

**3~ ASSEMBLY.** Use a jump ring to string 1 simple loop of the hoop, the free ends of the dangles in the order they were created, and the remaining simple loop of the hoop.

## crystal cascade

### MATERIALS

8 jonquil satin 4mm crystal bicones

3 light olivine 4mm crystal bicones

2 erinite 6mm crystal rounds

5 crystal golden shadow 14mm crystal rings

1 crystal golden shadow 30mm crystal ring

7 gold-filled 1½" (38mm) head pins

9 gold-filled 3mm jump rings

13" (33 cm) of gold-filled 2mm round chain

2" (5 cm) of gold-filled 1.6mm double-cable round chain

5" (12.5 cm) of gold-filled 24-gauge wire

**1~ PENDANT HANGERS.** Use loops of chain and wrapped-loop links to attach two 14mm rings to the top of the pendant (work the strands of your necklace off of these rings):

**Link:** Use 2½" (6.5 cm) of wire to form a large wrapped loop that attaches to one 14mm ring; string 1 jonquil satin bicone, 1 erinite round, and 1 jonquil satin bicone. Form a wrapped loop to complete the link.

**Chain loops:** Use 1" (2.5 cm) of 1.6mm chain to string the 30mm ring; attach a jump ring to both ends of chain and the free end of the previously formed link.

Repeat entire step to form a second pendant hanger.

**2~ DANGLES.** Form dangles made of chains and crystals between the two hangers, from left to right in the following order:

**Short crystal-ring dangle:** Use 2" (5 cm) of 2mm chain to string one 14mm ring and the 30mm ring. Use 1 jump ring to attach both ends of the chain to a link in the middle of the chain, forming loops around both crystal rings.

**Short chain dangle:** Use 2" (5 cm) of 2mm chain to string the 30mm ring and use a jump ring to attach the end to a chain link that is about ½" (1.3 cm) from the end, forming a loop. Use a head pin to string 1 jonquil satin bicone and form a simple loop that attaches to the free end of the chain.

**Long crystal-ring dangle:** Use 3¾" (9.5 cm) of 2mm chain to string one 14mm ring and use a jump ring to attach the end to a chain link that is about ½" (1.3 cm) away, forming a loop.

Pass the other end of the chain through the 30mm ring and use a jump ring to attach the end to a chain link that is about 1" (2.5 cm) away, forming a loop.

**Long chain dangle:** Repeat as for the short chain dangle, using 2½" (6.5 cm) of 2mm chain.

**Medium crystal-ring dangle:** Repeat as for the long crystal-ring dangle, using 2½" (6.5 cm) of 2mm chain.

**Bicones:** Use each remaining head pin to string 1 jonquil satin or 1 light olivine bicone; form simple loops that attach to the chains, placing them at random.

## shimmer & shell

### MATERIALS

8 bronze 4x7mm faceted pressed-glass tapered ovals

6 labradorite 4mm faceted rounds

1 cream/bronze engraved 36mm top-drilled shell donut

4 gold-filled 1½" (38mm) head pins

8" (20.5 cm) of gold-filled 2mm round chain

4" (10 cm) of gold-filled 24-gauge wire

1~ **DANGLES.** Use a head pin to string 1 oval and 1 faceted round. Use 1¼" (3.2 cm) of chain to string the large hole of the donut and use the head pin to form a wrapped loop that attaches to both ends of chain, forming a loop around the donut. Repeat entire step using 1¾" (4.5 cm), 1½" (3.8 cm), and 1¼" (3.2 cm) pieces of chain, respectively, for the 3 remaining dangles.

2~ **PENDANT HANGERS.** To work strands off of the focal, pass 1" (2.5 cm) of chain through the top-drilled hole in the donut; use 2" (5 cm) of wire to form a wrapped loop that attaches to both ends of chain. String 1 oval, 1 faceted round, and 1 oval and form a wrapped loop to complete a link.

Repeat entire step to form a second pendant hanger.

***Note:*** *If you find it difficult to pass the second chain through the top-drilled hole, hold the very end of the chain between your thumb and index finger and push into the hole until at least one link can be seen from the other side; pass a scrap piece of wire through the link and use it to help pull the chain through the hole.*

## lovely links

{see pendant on p. 10 and at right}

### MATERIALS

22 gold-lined clear 5x3mm faceted pressed-glass rondelles

3 jade 6x10mm faceted teardrops

2 natural brass 10mm detached round chain links

8" (20.5 cm) of gold-filled 24-gauge wire

1~ **LINK.** Use 2" (5 cm) of wire to form a wrapped loop that attaches to 1 chain link; string 1 rondelle. Form a wrapped loop that attaches to the remaining chain link (this completes a wrapped-loop link).

2~ **DANGLES.** Use 2" (5 cm) of wire to string 1 teardrop and form a wrapped-loop bail that attaches to 1 chain link. Repeat to attach another dangle to the same chain link.

Use 2" (5 cm) of wire to string 1 teardrop and 1 rondelle, forming a trapped-bead bail with a wrapped loop that attaches to the chain link between the two previously formed dangles.

3~ **FINISHING.** For a suggestion on how to incorporate this pendant into a necklace, see the sidebar at right.

*Attach copper satin .018 beading wire to the top chain link of the **lovely links** pendant using crimp beads and string gold-lined clear rondelles, rutilated quartz 8mm faceted rounds with natural brass 7×3mm patterned bead caps, and additional gold-lined clear rondelles.*

## stringing *suggestion*

# etch-a-bead

Nature comes alive in these etched pendants and beads. By using stickers that are temporarily applied to glass and etching cream, the outlines of the stickers are permanently transferred to the glass. When the pendants are washed, the smooth glass that was protected by the stickers is magically revealed.

## *etched pendants*

### MATERIALS

Assorted 10–30mm glass pendants
 and briolettes

Assorted stickers in the shapes of stars, hearts,
 deer, owls, rabbits, birds, and butterflies

Masking tape (optional)

Glass etching cream

Newspaper

Rubber or vinyl gloves

1~ **PREPARATION.** Working in a well-ventilated area and near a sink, cover your work surface with newspaper. Wash all pendants with soapy water, rinse, and dry well.

2~ **STICKERS.** Choose the design you wish to etch on the glass, keeping in mind that the sticker will preserve the smooth surface of the glass and the area around the sticker will be etched.

  Apply stickers and burnish with the popsicle stick, being careful not to tear the edges of the sticker; do not worry if the sticker extends beyond the edges of the glass.

3~ **ETCHING CREAM.** Don your gloves and use the paintbrush to add a thick layer of cream. Begin by piling a liberal amount in the center of the pendant, on top of the sticker(s), and gently spread it out across the pendant, making sure to not damage the sticker, and spreading the cream out to the edges of the pendant (if you spread the cream beyond the top surface of the pendant, the edges will also be etched; if you don't feel that you have a steady enough hand to spread the cream out to the edges evenly, protect the edges with masking tape).

4~ **FINISHING.** After the entire surface of the pendant has been covered, wait 60 to 90 seconds. Completely rinse the cream off under cold water; turn the water to hot to rinse off the sticker(s). Dry pendants thoroughly.

crystal disco
duo

forest friend

garnet
asymmetry

tears of joy

**TOOLBOX**
Wire cutters
Round-nose pliers
Chain-nose pliers
Flat-nose pliers (optional)

# classy coils

Make simple frames fancy by coiling them with wire and gemstone beads. Experiment with colored wire and finish the design by filling the frames with charms and dangles. You'll have a classy coil to show off in no time.

## *garnet asymmetry*

### MATERIALS

17 garnet 4mm rounds
1 sterling silver 38mm round bead frame
30" (76 cm) of gold-filled 24-gauge wire

1 ~ **WRAPPING.** Fold the wire in half and use one end to string the bead frame. Pull the wire ends so that the inside of the fold is tight against the frame.
**First half:** Holding the wire fold in place, wrap one end of the wire around one half of the frame, working toward the other side of the frame and leaving about ¹/₈" (3 mm) between the wraps.
**Second half:** Use the other end of the wire to string 1 garnet. Slide the garnet down and wrap the wire around the frame to center the garnet on the outside edge. Without stringing a garnet, make another wrap close to the previous wrap (you will have twice as many wraps on this half of the frame).

Repeat to cover the second half of the frame, adding garnets and wrapping until you meet the tail of the previous wire on the outside edge of the frame; bend the tail away from the frame at a 90° angle.

2 ~ **FINISHING.** Form a wrapped-loop link with bail that is embellished with a garnet:
**First tail:** Wrap the tail from the first half of the frame two to three times around the base of the second wire tail; trim.
**Second tail:** Use the remaining wire to string 1 garnet and form a wrapped loop.

## forest friend

{ see pendant on p. 16 and at far right}

**MATERIALS**

1 white 30mm bone bead frame

1 fine silver 15x20mm deer charm

1 antique brass 10mm jump ring

22" (56 cm) of gunmetal 20-gauge craft wire

**1~ WRAPPING.** Repeat as for Garnet Asymmetry, omitting the garnets and varying the space between the wires for a free-form look.

**2~ FINISHING.** Finish the wire tails and fill the center of the bead frame:

**Bail:** Use the wire tails to form a wrapped-loop bail at the top of the bead frame.

**Charm:** Open the jump ring wide and string the bead frame, passing it under the wrapped-loop bail. String the charm before closing.

**Stringing:** For a suggestion on how to incorporate this pendant into a necklace, see the sidebar at far right.

## crystal disco duo

**MATERIALS**

2 crystal tabac 14mm crystal rings

1 sterling silver 16x36mm bead frame

1 sterling silver 10mm jump ring

18" (45.5 cm) of navy blue 20-gauge craft wire

4½" (11.5 cm) of sterling silver 20-gauge wire

**1~ WRAPPING.** Cut the blue craft wire in half.

**Bottom half:** Starting with at least a 1" (2.5 cm) tail at one side of the frame, wrap one blue wire around the bottom half until covered; trim the wire tails.

**Top half:** Repeat for the top half of the frame, using the remaining blue wire; you will need to pass a wire through the frame's top hole in Step 2, so leave a small space in the center.

**2~ FINISHING.** Use the silver wire to make the hanging device and finish with the crystals:

**Link:** Use the silver wire to form a large wrapped loop that attaches to one crystal ring. String the frame, passing the wire through the top half of the frame from the inside out. Form a wrapped loop.

**Crystals:** Use the jump ring to join the crystals.

---

### ❧ tips

➤ *If using bead frames that differ in size and shape from the ones used here, be sure to use a little more wire than you think you need.*

➤ *The more the wire is manipulated, the harder it becomes so be sure to wrap carefully the first time.*

➤ *Don't worry if the wraps aren't perfectly spaced. You can use flat-nose pliers to carefully slide them along the frame into the desired position after the pendant is finished.*

## tears of joy

{see pendant on p. 16 and at lower right}

**MATERIALS**

1 topaz 2mm crystal bicone

1 crystal clear 10mm crystal round

1 silver 10x14mm hammered cone

1 sterling silver 22x32mm teardrop bead frame

1 gold-filled 1½" (38mm) head pin with ball end

1 gold-filled 6mm jump ring

18" (45.5 cm) of gold-filled 20-gauge wire

1 ~ **WRAPPING.** Repeat as for Garnet Asymmetry, omitting the garnets and leaving about ¹/₁₆" (2 mm) between wraps.

2 ~ **FINISHING.** Finish the wire tails and fill the center of the bead frame:

**Bail:** Use the wire tails to form a wrapped-loop bail at the top of the bead frame.

**Dangle:** Use the head pin to string the 8mm round, hammered cone, and bicone; form a simple loop.

**Jump ring:** Open the jump ring wide and string the bead frame, passing it under the wrapped-loop bail. String the dangle before closing.

**Stringing:** For a suggestion on how to incorporate this pendant into a necklace, see the sidebar at right.

◄ *String the* **forest friend** *pendant with pale mint green 11mm vintage Lucite rounds, pearly white size 8° seed beads, pyrite 4mm cubes, and blue/mint 5mm fire-polished rounds.*

## stringing *suggestions*

▼ *String the* **tears of joy** *pendant with pineapple quartz 6mm faceted rounds, sterling silver 10mm bead frames, and gold size 15° charlottes. Since the wire will be exposed when rounds are strung inside the frames, copper satin .018 beading wire is recommended.*

# fantastic plastic

Trace it, color it, bake it, wear it—it's really that easy. With patterns taken from a book of copyright-free images, anyone can draw like a well-trained artist. Wear them alone or layer with other favorite pendants.

## *plastic pendants*

### MATERIALS

1 sheet of frosted clear Shrinky Dinks Shrinkable Plastic
1 sheet of crystal clear plastic Grafix Shrink Film
Black fine-point and extra-fine-point permanent markers
Colored pencils
Parchment paper

**1 ~ PREPARATION.** Prepare the plastic for baking:

**Cutting:** Cut a piece of plastic that is three times larger than the desired finished size of your pendant. For example, for a pendant that is about 1¼" (3.2 cm) square, make the original about 3¾" (9.5 cm) square. If cutting shapes with sharp edges, use the scissors to round the corners slightly.

Use the crystal clear plastic if working only with markers; use the frosted clear plastic if working with colored pencils. If you only have the crystal clear plastic but wish to use colored pencils, roughen one side with sandpaper.

**Outlining:** Find a copyright-free image that you wish to use for your pendant and lay the plastic over the image (if needed, first enlarge or reduce the image using a photocopier, keeping in mind that the pattern will be greatly reduced when baked).

If working with frosted or sanded plastic, make sure the rough side is face up. Use the markers to trace over the outlines of the image. Don't worry if your lines aren't perfect, the imperfections will not show after the plastic has shrunk.

**Coloring:** If desired, use the colored pencils to color the plastic. The color will intensify when the plastic is shrunk—a little bit of color goes a long way.

**Hanging:** Use the hole punch to make holes for the hanging device before baking.

2~ **BAKING.** Preheat the oven to 325°F.

**Preparation:** Line the baking tray with parchment paper and lay the plastic pieces at least 1½" (3.8 cm) apart, drawing side up. The plastic will temporarily curl and twist during the baking cycle but will flatten back out before baking is complete.

If working with a large sheet of crystal clear plastic, the ends may curl so much that they touch the center of the pendant; to avoid harming your image, one manufacturer suggests placing a small piece of parchment paper on top of the center of the drawing while baking.

**Shrinking:** Bake for 2 to 5 minutes. Once the piece flattens back to its original shape after curling, bake it for 20 to 30 more seconds. Remove the tray from the oven.

If any of the pieces need additional flattening once removed, quickly cover them with a piece of parchment paper and flatten with a book or the bottom of a glass while still hot.

3~ **FINISHING.** For suggestions on how to incorporate these pendants into necklaces, see the sidebar at right.

## 🌿 Tips

➤ *Bake similar-size pieces at the same time so that all of the pieces are finished baking at about the same size and none of the small pieces get over baked.*

➤ *The copyright-free images used for the pendants shown here appear in* 4000 Flower & Plant Motifs *by Graham Leslie McCallum (Bastford: London, 2004)—a highly recommended book!*

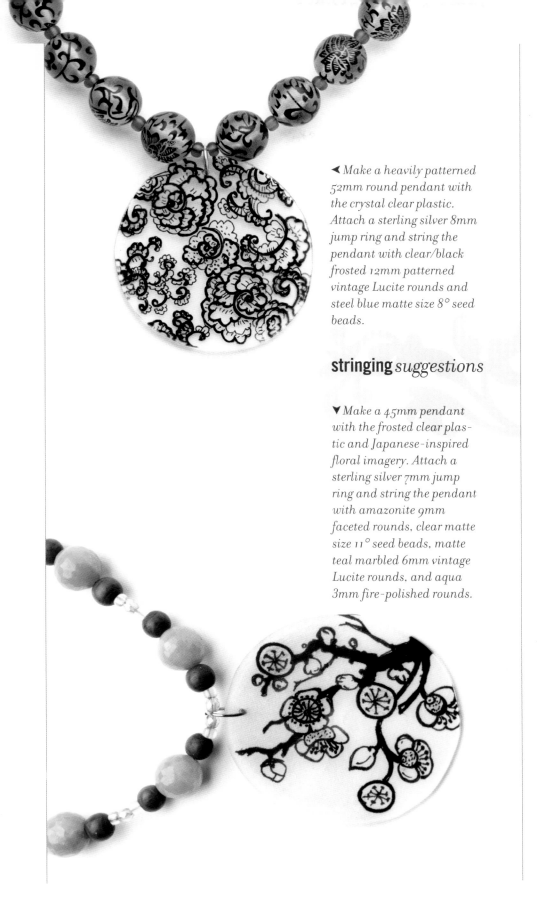

◄ *Make a heavily patterned 52mm round pendant with the crystal clear plastic. Attach a sterling silver 8mm jump ring and string the pendant with clear/black frosted 12mm patterned vintage Lucite rounds and steel blue matte size 8° seed beads.*

## stringing *suggestions*

▼ *Make a 45mm pendant with the frosted clear plastic and Japanese-inspired floral imagery. Attach a sterling silver 7mm jump ring and string the pendant with amazonite 9mm faceted rounds, clear matte size 11° seed beads, matte teal marbled 6mm vintage Lucite rounds, and aqua 3mm fire-polished rounds.*

*autumn window*

*rings & raindrops*

*evening elegance*

*bird cage*

*mod metal*

**TOOLBOX**
Wire cutters
Round-nose pliers
Chain-nose pliers

# flirty frames

Contain yourself! Turn plain bead frames and hoops into fabulous and flirty focal pieces. Be bold when selecting beads, the outside frames will visually contain them no matter how funky the mix.

## *rings & raindrops*

### MATERIALS

5 aquamarine 5x3mm faceted rondelles

7 labradorite 6x9mm faceted briolettes

1 Thai silver 30mm ring

1 Thai silver 50mm ring

2 sterling silver 3mm jump rings

6 sterling silver 6mm jump rings

1 sterling silver 8mm jump ring

2" (5 cm) of sterling silver 2mm round chain

10½" (26.5 cm) of silver 26-gauge craft wire

1~ **RINGS.** Use the 8mm jump ring to string the holes of both Thai silver rings. Attach a 6mm jump ring to the top of the largest ring.

2~ **CHAINS.** Cut one 1½" (3.8 cm) and one ³⁄₈" (1 cm) piece of chain and embellish as follows:

**Labradorite briolettes:** Use 1½" (3.8 cm) of wire to string 1 labradorite briolette and form a wrapped-loop bail that attaches to 1 link on one end of the long piece of chain (this will be considered the first link). Repeat to attach 4 additional bails to the desired chain links.

Repeat to attach 1 labradorite briolette wrapped-loop bail to the first and last links of the short piece of chain. Set this chain aside.

**Aquamarine rondelles:** Use one 6mm jump ring to string 1 aquamarine rondelle and attach to a desired link of the long chain. Repeat to add 4 additional jump rings/rondelles to the desired chain links of the long chain.

3~ **JOINING.** Use a 3mm jump ring to attach the last link of the long chain to the 8mm jump ring, in front of the Thai silver rings. Repeat to attach the last link of the short chain to the 8mm jump ring.

4~ **FINISHING.** For a suggestion on how to incorporate this pendant into a necklace, see the sidebar on p. 27.

## *autumn window*

### MATERIALS

2 pale topaz 4mm fire-polished rounds

1 green matte 7x3mm pressed-glass flower

3 matte 10x22mm pressed-glass leaves with attached simple loops in green, yellow, and red

1" (2.5 cm) of gold-filled 1.5mm round chain

2" (5 cm) of gold-filled 24-gauge wire

1~ **DANGLES.** Make 3 dangles:
**Red dangle:** Open the red leaf's simple loop and string ½" (1.3 cm) of chain. Set aside.
**Yellow dangle:** Open the yellow leaf's simple loop and string ¼" (6mm) of chain. Set aside.
**Green dangle:** Open the green leaf's simple loop and string ⅛" (3mm) of chain. Set aside.

2~ **FRAME ASSEMBLY.** Use the wire to form a wrapped loop; string 1 fire-polished round, the pressed-glass flower, and 1 fire-polished round. Form a wrapped loop that attaches to the free end of each dangle's chain and one corner of the brass frame.

## *mod metal*

### MATERIALS

1 sterling silver 9mm (small) round bead frame

1 gold-filled 11mm (small) round bead frame

1 sterling silver 15x22mm (small) rectangle bead frame

1 gold-filled 23mm (large) round bead frame

1 sterling silver 30x54mm (large) frame with soldered rings

2 sterling silver 6mm jump rings

2 gold-filled 1" (25mm) head pins

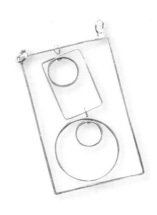

1~ **INSIDE FRAMES.** Assemble the inside frames in two pieces before joining them together:
**Rectangle inside frame:** Working from the inside out, use a head pin to string the small gold round bead frame and the small silver rectangle bead frame. Form a simple loop and set aside.
**Round inside frame:** Working from the inside out, use a head pin to string the small silver round bead frame and the large gold round bead frame. Form a simple loop and set aside.

2~ **ASSEMBLY.** Open the simple loop of the rectangle inside frame and attach it to the top of the large silver frame, between the soldered rings. Open the simple loop of the round inside frame and attach it to the bottom of the rectangle inside frame.

3~ **FINISHING.** Attach a jump ring to each of the large frame's soldered rings. If the inside frames do not hang freely inside of the large frame, shorten the simple loops by gently flattening them top to bottom.

## *evening elegance*

### MATERIALS

6 dusty rose/bronze 3mm fire-polished rounds

3 black 12x22mm vintage pressed-glass leaves with attached wires

1 gold-filled 15x22mm (small) rectangle bead frame

1 gold-filled 16x36mm (large) rectangle bead frame

1~ **LARGE FRAME.** Use 1 leaf wire to string 3 fire-polished rounds. Use a second leaf wire to string 1 fire-polished round.

Pass the first leaf wire through the bead just strung and continue to use the two leaf wires as if they were one: String one side of the large rectangle frame (from the inside out) and 1 fire-polished round; form a wrapped loop.

2~ **SMALL FRAME.** Use 1 leaf wire to string one side of the small bead frame (from the inside out), 1 fire-polished round, and the bottom of the large bead frame. Trim the leaf wire to 1" (2.5 cm) and use round-nose pliers to coil the end down for several turns.

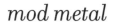

## bird cage

**MATERIALS**

2 rose 3mm fire-polished rounds

3 green 4mm fire-polished rounds

3 rose 4mm fire-polished rounds

3 turquoise mottled 5x9mm teardrops

4 clear/amber/green mottled 5x16mm daggers

3 smoky topaz 8x6mm rondelles

1 pewter 22x8mm bird bead

1 brass 50mm round frame

1 brass 65mm square frame with rounded corners

9 antique brass 6mm jump rings

4 antique brass 8mm jump rings

7 antique brass 1½" (38mm) head pins

6" (15 cm) of antique brass assorted 2–6mm oval chain

**1~ CHAIN.** Cut the chain(s) into the following lengths: ½" (1.3 cm), 1½" (3.8 cm), 1¾" (4.5 cm), and 2" (5 cm). Embellish as follows:

**Bird:** Use a head pin to string 1 rose 4mm fire-polished round, the bird bead, and 1 green 4mm fire-polished round; form a wrapped loop that attaches to the end of the ½" (1.3 cm) piece of chain. Set aside.

**Topaz rondelles:** Use one 8mm jump ring to string 1 topaz rondelle and attach it to the end of the 1¾" (4.5 cm) piece of chain. Repeat using 8mm jump rings to add 2 more evenly spaced topaz rondelles to the chain.

Use a head pin to string one of the remaining fire-polished rounds; form a simple loop that attaches to one of the chain's links. Repeat using the 5 remaining head pins and fire-polished rounds, placing them on the chain in the order desired. Set aside.

**Teardrops:** Use one 6mm jump ring to string 1 teardrop and attach it to the end of the 1½" (3.8 cm) piece of chain. Repeat to attach the 2 remaining teardrops to the desired chain links. Set aside.

**Daggers:** Use one 6mm jump ring to string 1 dagger and attach it to the end of the 2" (5 cm) piece of chain. Repeat to attach the 3 remaining daggers to the chain in the order desired. Set aside.

**2~ FRAME ASSEMBLY.** Hold the round brass frame inside of the square frame. Use one 6mm jump ring to attach the frames along one side of the square.

Use a second jump ring to join the frames along an adjacent side of the square so that the round frame hangs from one corner of the square frame.

**3~ CHAIN ASSEMBLY.** Use an 8mm jump ring to string the free ends of the chains and square frame in the following order: bird chain, topaz-rondelles chain, the corner of the square frame that is centered above the round frame, teardrops chain, and daggers chain.

### stringing *suggestion*

*Attach the 6mm jump ring at the top of the* **rings & raindrops** *pendant to sterling silver 9×11mm oval chain. Use 5mm jump rings to string additional aquamarine 5×3mm faceted rondelles and attach them to links of the chain.*

# impressionable clay

From floral to abstract, any favorite rubber stamp turns balls of polymer clay into fabulously textured beads. For an even richer look, experiment with color mixes and finishes. Remember, you only have one chance to make a first impression.

## *clay pendants*

### MATERIALS

Assorted rubber stamps

2mm crystal bicones or other small accent beads (optional)

Assorted colors of Fimo polymer modeling clay, including purple, pink, glittery white, tan, glittery gold, green, and brown

Brick red and brown dye-based stamp pads

Amazing Glaze resin powder (optional)

Antique yellow embossing powder (optional)

Assorted gunmetal, bright copper, and silver 2" (50mm) head pins and eye pins and/or 18- to 22-gauge wire

Assorted silver and antique brass and copper 8–12mm round and rectangle jump rings

Ballpoint pen

Masking tape

Waxed paper

Parchment paper

G-S Hypo Cement

Baking sheet

Large head pin for forming holes in clay

Clear glass flat-bottomed cup

1 ~ **WORKSPACE.** Though the clay is nontoxic, it's a good idea to cover your working surface with waxed paper and tape the edges down. Wrap the rolling pin with waxed paper and tape in place.

2 ~ **MIX COLORS.** Custom colors can be made by mixing together different-colored pieces of clay. The more you experiment with colors, the sooner you'll be able to see what colors mix together best.

If you are working with a pasta machine, pass the clays through the machine several times, folding the clays between each pass to blend the colors.

If you do not have a pasta machine, simply press small pieces of clay together and roll between the palms of your hands (or on the covered work surface with the rolling pin) to combine, folding and tearing the clay as necessary to blend the colors. Add dark colors in small amounts—a little bit goes a long way.

3~ **INKING THE STAMP.** Prepare the stamp by lightly pressing it into the brown and brick red ink pads. Lay the stamp face up on your work surface.

4~ **SHAPING AND STAMPING.** Use the following guidelines when stamping:

**Coins and ovals:** To make coin-shaped pendants, use the palms of your hands to make a ¼–½" (6mm–1.3cm) ball. For an oblong pendant, gently shape the ball into a thick oval/egglike shape.

**Squares and rectangles:** If a square pendant is desired, form a ball; if a rectangle pendant is desired, roll the clay into a cylinder.

After pressing the clay in the following stamping step, use the razor blade to cut the pendant to the desired shape. Use your index finger to smooth the edges and round the corners.

**Embellishment:** If you wish to bake embellishments into the pendants, lay the crystals (or other small accent beads) in the grooves of the stamp.

**Stamping:** While the clay is still warm from body heat, lay it on the stamp, gently cover it with a small piece of waxed paper, and press with the bottom of the glass to flatten.

To ensure that you are pressing with even pressure, look down through the glass so you can watch the shape being formed. Press until desired thickness is achieved (⅛–¼" [3–6mm]). Lift the glass and remove the waxed paper.

To release the pendant from the stamp, hold the stamp in one hand and the clay in the other and gently wiggle the clay until it releases; reshape the clay as needed.

If the edges of the clay cracked as you flattened the pendant, gently rub the edges with your index finger to smooth and seal the cracks.

**Texturizing:** To add a rustic look, lightly dust with the yellow embossing powder.

5~ **MAKE HOLES.** Form holes in the clay before baking; choose from the following hanging variations:

**Small holes:** For small horizontal holes that pierce the face of the pendant, press the large head pin into the clay, and move the head pin in a circular motion to enlarge the hole.

To form small vertical holes on the top edge of the pendant that will be filled with short eye pins or wire, use the large head pin to push ¼–½" (6 mm–1.3 cm) straight into the thick-

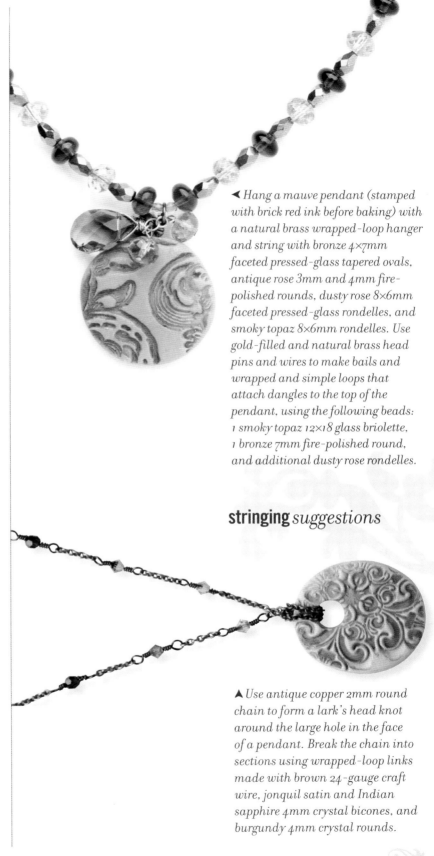

ness of the pendant, being sure to keep the pin parallel to the sides of the pendant.

Make a vertical hole through the entire thickness of the pendant, from bottom to top, if you wish to later string the pendant on a long head pin.

**Large holes:** For large horizontal holes that pierce the face of the pendant, lay the pendant on a parchment or waxed paper–covered surface. Determine the top of the pendant, disassemble the ballpoint pen, and press the large outer tube of the pen down through the face of the pendant, near an edge.

Remove the pen (the removed clay will be inside the tube of the pen). Do not worry if this distorts the pendant; simply reshape the pendant and gently smooth the edge of the hole on the back of the pendant.

**6~ BAKING.** Place the pendants on parchment paper on a baking sheet. Bake the pendants according to the clay manufacturer's directions, or at 265°F for about 30 minutes.

◄ *Hang a mauve pendant (stamped with brick red ink before baking) with a natural brass wrapped-loop hanger and string with bronze 4×7mm faceted pressed-glass tapered ovals, antique rose 3mm and 4mm fire-polished rounds, dusty rose 8×6mm faceted pressed-glass rondelles, and smoky topaz 8×6mm rondelles. Use gold-filled and natural brass head pins and wires to make bails and wrapped and simple loops that attach dangles to the top of the pendant, using the following beads: 1 smoky topaz 12×18 glass briolette, 1 bronze 7mm fire-polished round, and additional dusty rose rondelles.*

## stringing *suggestions*

▲ *Use antique copper 2mm round chain to form a lark's head knot around the large hole in the face of a pendant. Break the chain into sections using wrapped-loop links made with brown 24-gauge craft wire, jonquil satin and Indian sapphire 4mm crystal bicones, and burgundy 4mm crystal rounds.*

**7~ GLAZING.** If you did not lightly dust the pendant with any yellow embossing powder before baking, you can still do so now.

To add shine (and seal any yellow embossing powder just added), sprinkle resin powder on top of the pendant and bake according to manufacturer's directions, about 3 to 5 minutes until melted (see p. 77 for more information on Amazing Glaze resin powder).

**8~ HANGING.** There are several ways you can add hanging devices to the pendants:
**Jump rings:** Use 1 or more jump ring(s) to string the pendant through a horizontal hole in the face of the pendant.
**Head pins/eye pins:** Coat the end of a shortened eye pin with cement and press into a vertical hole on the top of the pendant. If using a head pin, string the pendant from the bottom to top and use the wire tail to form a simple or wrapped loop at the top.
**Wrapped-loop hanger:** Use 2" (5 cm) of 18- to 22-gauge wire to form a wrapped loop. Coat the end of the wire with cement and press into a vertical hole of the pendant.
**Wrapped-loop bail:** Pass 2 to 3" (5–7.5 cm) of 18- to 22-gauge wire through a horizontal hole in the face of the pendant and form a wrapped-loop bail.

**9 ~ FINISHING.** For suggestions on how to incorporte these pendants in necklaces, see the sidebar on p. 31.

# élan lace

You can also embellish clay pendants by transferring photocopied images onto the surface. For the pendants seen here, scraps of lace were used to bring textile traditions together with new technology.

### IMAGE-TRANSFER PENDANTS

In addition to the materials and tools listed on p. 29 (excluding the rubber stamps, stamp pads, embossing powder, and ballpoint pen) you will need the following:

### TOOLBOX

Butter knife with smooth handle

Pin or pair of fine tweezers

Toner-based photocopy machine

### MATERIALS

Fimo polymer modeling clay in glittery white, blue, teal, and sea foam green

White and black scraps of lace

8½ x 11" (21.5 x 28 cm) black piece of paper

Masking or clear tape

Nail polish remover

Cotton swabs

**1~ PHOTOCOPY.** Lay the white lace on the bed of a toner-based copy machine, cover with the black paper, and make several copies, enlarging and reducing the scale of the lace as desired. Repeat using the black lace and omitting the black piece of paper.

**2~ PENDANTS.** Mix and shape the clay and make holes in the pendants according to pp. 29–31.

**3~ APPLY IMAGE.** Before baking the pendants, cut the images to be transferred to the shape of the pendant. Use a cotton swab to wet the pendant with polish remover. Lay the photocopy face down on the pendant.

To transfer the image, gently rub the back of the paper with the end of the butter knife's handle; be sure not to move the paper or the image will be blurred. Wet the pendant/paper again with polish remover. If the design has fine lines, gently rub them again, making sure not to distort the pendant. Wait 1 to 2 minutes and use the pin or tweezers to gently lift the paper from the pendant.

Don't worry if much of the paper remains on the surface: Go to the sink, turn the faucet so that only small drips of water come out, wet the pendant, and slowly rub the pendant to remove the excess paper pulp.

Continue cleaning the surface until all paper is gone; if any paper remains, it will show after baking and will be harder to remove. For baking, glazing, and hanging instructions, see pp. 31–32.

### Tip

*Stick with Fimo brand when transferring images to the clay, the other brands tested did not work as well, producing a poorly transferred image.*

TOOLBOX
Wire cutters
Round-nose pliers
Chain-nose pliers

# top it off

With just a little practice, wrapped-loop bails are surprisingly easy to work up, and they instantly turn any briolette, teardrop, or crystal into a customized pendant. Top some with a tinge of fringe for delightful flair.

## *wire-wrapped pendants*

### MATERIALS

Assorted stone, glass, or crystal 7–42mm faceted and smooth briolettes, teardrops, daggers, and pendants

Liver of sulfur, baking soda, polishing cloth, and/or #0000 steel wool (optional)

Assorted lengths (10–18" [25.5–45.5 cm]) of 24- to 20-gauge wire for each bead in light copper, dark copper, gunmetal, gold-filled, and/or sterling silver

1 ~ **BEGIN.** Use 10–12" (25.5–30.5 cm) of wire if working with a small bead and 16–18" (40.5–45.5 cm) of wire if working with a large bead. String 1 bead, positioning the bead so that it is about 2" (5 cm) from one end of the wire. Bend both wire ends toward the center top of the bead, forming a triangle. Use the chain-nose pliers to bend the long wire straight up at the top of the bead {Fig. 1}.

**First wraps:** Wrap the short wire around the long wire; if you have trouble holding the wires and bead while wrapping, swing the top of the bead out of the triangle formed and hold the triangle with the round-nose pliers {Fig. 2}. Trim the short wire after forming the wraps.

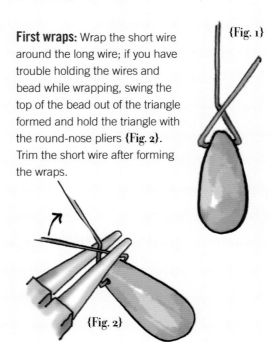

{Fig. 1}

{Fig. 2}

**stringing** *suggestion*

### SWEET EMERALD EARRINGS

*Use 10" (25.5 cm) of sterling silver 24-gauge wire and 1 amazonite 8×10mm faceted teardrop to form a wrapped-loop bail that attaches to one end of ⅝" (1.5 cm) of sterling silver 2mm round chain. Use an ear wire to string the free end of the chain. Use sterling silver 1½" (3.8 cm) flat- and ball-end head pins and chrysolite, peridot, erinite, emerald, and olivine 4mm bicone crystals to form wrapped-loop dangles, attaching them to the desired links of chain. Repeat for a second earring.*

**Loop:** Hold the first wraps with the chain-nose pliers and bend the remaining wire down to one side at a 90° angle. Use the round-nose pliers to form a loop {Fig. 3}.

{Fig. 3}

**Final wraps:** Hold the loop in the chain-nose pliers and wrap the wire down over the first wraps. Continue to wrap over the top of the bead, holding the bead so that the top is centered under the first wraps.

After the top of the bead has been covered with a few wraps, you may find it easier to remove the pliers and finish wrapping the wire by hand, rotating the bead to help keep tension on the wire. Trim the wire when the desired amount of bead is covered {Fig. 4}.

2~ **FINISHING.** If desired, decorate the pendants using the following methods:
**Coloring:** To oxidize the silver pendants using liver of sulfur, see p. 103. Dipping the pendants completely in a solution of liver of sulfur will not harm the stones.
**Dangles:** Use head pins to string beads and form wrapped- or simple-loop dangles that attach to the top loop of the pendant.

The clear crystal dagger shown on p. 34 is topped by simple loop dangles made of sterling silver 1" (25mm) head pins with clear 4mm crystal rounds and Indian sapphire satin and clear satin AB 4mm crystal bicones. The entire pendant was treated with liver of sulfur.
**Stringing:** For suggestions on how to incorporate these pendants into necklaces, see the sidebar at right.

{Fig. 4}

◄ *Form a bail on top of a spotted yellow turquoise 30×40mm briolette using sterling silver 24-gauge wire. String the pendant with moss green marbled 9mm vintage Lucite rounds, matte teal marbled 6mm vintage Lucite rounds, and light topaz 4mm fire-polished rounds.*

## stringing *suggestions*

▼ *Form a bail on top of a chita 22×30mm briolette using brown 24-gauge craft wire. String the pendant with amber/green 7×8mm pressed-glass cathedral beads, honey opal 4mm rounds, copper 3mm rounds, and light green/brown 4mm fire-polished rounds. Top the pendant with 8 wrapped-loop dangles made with antique copper 1½" (38mm) head pins and additional copper, honey opal, and fire-polished rounds.*

TOOLBOX

Circle template

Fabric-marking pencil

$1/8$" (3mm) metal vertical hole
  punch and eyelet setter
  with $1/8$" (3mm) setting tip

Cutting mat

Hammer

Size 3 embroidery needle
  or size 22 chenille needle

Sewing thread

Iron and ironing board

Scissors

Acid-free white craft glue
  (optional)

# patchwork panache

Fabric, stamps, ink, needles, thread—it's time to use all of your craft-room goodies to create these surprisingly quick-to-make, layered accessories. The optional stitched embellishment uses the easiest stitch of them all, the running stitch.

## *patchwork pendants*

### MATERIALS

Dye-based permanent ink pad

Stamp set with abstract, floral, and/or bird patterns

Scraps of cotton fabric, ribbon, and rickrack

Felt to match fabrics

Fusible web (see sidebar on p. 75)

Assorted copper, brass, and silver 5–12mm round
  and rectangle jump rings

$1/8$" (3mm) eyelets in colors to complement fabrics

6-strand cotton embroidery thread

Craft glue (optional)

1~ **CENTRAL IMAGE.** Prepare the central image before building the base layers:

**Stamping:** Use inked stamps to decorate scraps of fabric for the focal point of your pendant. If working with patterned fabric, consider stamping on the backside—this will make the pattern more subtle and the stamp more prominent.

**Cutting and fusing:** Trim the image to the desired size, using the circle template and fabric-marking pencil as a guide.

Cut a piece of fusible web about ¼" (6 mm) smaller than the image and use the iron to adhere the fusible web to the back of the image, according

### ❧Tips

➤ *Use a press cloth and turn the iron temperature down when working with synthetics like ribbon.*

➤ *Ironing will help heat-set (make permanent) the dye of the stamp.*

➤ *To avoid crushing dimensional items when ironing, press them face down on a clean, fluffy terrycloth towel.*

to manufacturer's directions. When cool, remove the web's paper backing and set aside.

*Note: If you do not wish for the fabric to fray, cut the fusible web to the exact shape and size of the fabrics.*

2~ **BACKING.** Join the layers of the pendant:
**Felt:** Cut the felt so that it is at least ½" (1.3 cm) larger than the general shape of the pendant's final dimensions. Cut a piece of fusible web that is the same size and fuse it to the felt; when cool, remove the paper backing.
**Background embellishment layers:** With the fusible side of the felt face up, cover with fabric scraps, ribbon, and rickrack, allowing the pieces to overhang the edges. Iron all pieces to fuse them to the felt and trim to the final pendant size.

It is best to have each embellishment layer touch the fusible web; however, if you have completely covered the felt with fabric but want to add more embellishments, it is okay to layer a narrow trim on top of the layers (the next process of fusing on the central image will help keep the trim intact).

**Attach central image:** First see Step 4 if finishing with a ribbon loop. With the fusible side face down on top of the embellishment layers, iron the central image to fuse all layers. If needed, use the craft glue to tack down any trims that did not get fused to the other embellishment layers.

3~ **EMBROIDERY.** If desired, embellish the layers with simple running stitch:
**Running stitch:** Tie a knot at the end of 20" (51 cm) of embroidery thread and bring the needle up near one of the fabric layers' borders.

Take the needle to the back of the felt about ¼" (6 mm) away from the base of the thread, along the line to be stitched, and bring the needle back up about ¼" (6 mm) away. {Fig. 1}. Repeat to complete the stitched line. Tie a knot at the base of the thread on the back of the pendant.

{Fig. 1}

**4~ HANGING.** Finish with one of these techniques:

**Ribbon loop:** Lay a ribbon vertically across the pendant (perpendicular to the central image) before attaching the central image in Step 2 but do not trim the top of it. Fold the excess ribbon at the top to the back and whipstitch the end to the felt to form a loop.

**Eyelets:** Lay the pendant on the cutting mat and position the hole punch at least 1/8" (3 mm) from the top edge of the fabric; strike with the hammer several times to form a hole.

Insert 1 eyelet in the hole from front to back. Turn the pendant over so that the tube end of the eyelet is facing up, center the eyelet setter over the eyelet, and strike with the hammer several times to set.

**Stringing:** For suggestions on how to incorporate these pendants into necklaces, see the sidebar at right.

◄ *Simply use green velvet ribbon to string a pendant finished with a ribbon loop; trim the velvet ribbon ends at an angle to help prevent fraying (if the ribbon is made of synthetic materials, you can also melt the edges slightly with a lighter).*

## stringing *suggestions*

▼ *Make a pendant with gold fabric that has been stamped with the image of a bird's nest, printed brown/pale blue fabric, and a brown eyelet. Attach an antique copper 9×12mm rectangle jump ring. String the pendant's jump ring with speckled brown/white size 8° seed beads, cream/brown 8×6mm faceted pressed-glass rondelles, and light blue mottled 5mm rounds.*

**TOOLBOX**

Heat tool

Tin snips or strong wire cutters

Craft knife with new
blade (optional)

Hammer (optional)

Cutting mat (optional)

Scissors

# it's in the cards

Embossed and embellished antique reproduction playing cards
quickly become narrative pendants when mounted in premade
frames. For added interest and dimension, layer the images with
brass wings, filigree pieces, bits of lace, and embossing powder.

## *collage pendants*

### MATERIALS

Antique copper and black patina 1½ x 1½" (3.8 x 3.8 cm)
Memory Frames, bright brass ⅞ x 1⅛" (2.2 x 3 cm)
frames, or sterling silver 1⅜ x 2½" (3.5 x 6.5 cm)
hinged-top 2-pane glass lockets

2 pieces of 1½ x 1½" (3.8 x 3.8 cm) Memory Glass for
each Memory Frame

Bright brass 20x15mm solid angel wings

Bright brass 53x30mm and 27x13mm filigree angel wings

Scraps of antique lace

Acid-free white craft glue

Deck of antique reproduction playing cards

Scrapbook paper (for backgrounds)

Antique copper 13–28mm filigree squares or circles

Dark copper embossing powder

Rubber stamps

Several sheets of white copier paper

Dye- and pigment-based ink stamp pads in brown

Fossilized leaves

Mod Podge (optional)

1~ **BACKGROUND.** Determine the size of the
collage needed to fill the fame and cut a card
(or piece of scrapbook paper) to size.

2~ **BORDERS.** Embellish the borders of the
background by embossing or adding lace
or leaves as desired:

**Embossing:** Lay out 3 sheets of paper. Stamp the
desired pattern around the edges of the card and
while the ink is still wet, move it to the next sheet
of paper, and cover with embossing powder.

Tap the card to remove any excess powder
and lay it on the next sheet of paper (the
excess embossing powder can be returned to
the container). Turn on the heat tool and slowly
move it back and forth over the card to melt
the embossing powder; allow to cool.

**Lace:** Trim the lace to the desired size and
glue the pieces along the borders of the card,
keeping in mind that the frame's edge will
cover part of the lace, so you may wish to use a
wider piece.

**Leaves:** Emboss a fossilized leaf as before; heat the embossing powder slowly and be cautious when using the heat tool to avoid burning the leaf. Trim to size and glue to the card.

**3~ CENTRAL IMAGE.** Adhere embellishments to the background as desired:
**Wings:** If working with solid, three-dimensional wings that are hollow on the back, fill with glue and allow to dry for 3 to 5 minutes before pressing onto the background.
**Figures:** Cut out figures from additional cards: When cutting out small pieces or working in areas that are too small for the tips of the scissors, lay the pieces on the cutting mat and carefully trim with the craft knife.
**Filigree:** If needed, hammer filigree pieces flat and use the tin snips (or strong wire cutters) to trim the piece to the desired size. Emboss if desired as before.

**4~ MOUNTING.** If the embellishments made the collage too thick and you are working with Memory Frames, do without the backing glass and use a thick piece of paper instead; cover the back with Mod Podge to protect. Mount pieces in the other frame styles according to manufacturer's directions.

**5~ FINISHING.** For suggestions on how to incorporate these pendants into necklaces, see the sidebar at right.

> *TIP*
> *For more info on embossing powders, tools, and techniques, see p. 51.*

◄ *Emboss the edges of an antique French reproduction playing card (with an image of an angel) with copper embossing powder and adhere a solid brass angel wing to the card's angel.*

*Mount in an antique copper Memory Frame with one piece of glass to protect the front; coat the back with Mod Podge.*

*Attach 1 antique copper jump ring to the top of the frame and string with brown striped 5mm vintage Lucite rounds, rose/topaz 3mm fire-polished rounds, dusty rose 8×6mm faceted pressed-glass rondelles, and gold size 15° charlottes.*

## stringing *suggestions*

▼ *Embellish the top and bottom edges of an antique French reproduction playing card (with an image of a woman doing needle-work) with vintage lace and mount in a bright brass ⅞ × 1⅛" (2.2 x 3 cm) frame.*

*Attach 1 antique brass jump ring to the top of the frame and string with smoky topaz 3×2mm faceted rondelles, white/yellow 4×3mm faceted pressed-glass rondelles, silver-lined orange matte size 11° seed beads, and citrine 4mm rounds.*

# locked in time

Use glass lockets to frame precious charms, seeds, paper, leaves, and other mementos. Give as a gift to commemorate an event or instinctively switch out a locket's contents depending on your mood or outfit.

**TOOLBOX**

Scissors

Pencil

Hammer, small flat-head screwdriver, wire cutters, and terry-cloth towel (optional)

**MATERIALS**

Sterling silver 22x40mm square, 24x42mm round, 21x42mm oval, or 20x40mm teardrop hinged glass lockets

Gunmetal and antique brass 35mm and 42mm "pocket watch" lockets

Scraps of paper or playing cards

Assorted collage items: bird and bee charms, jump rings, antique watch parts, seed beads, dried seeds, sequins, dried leaves, playing cards, and micro (1mm) glass balls

Acid-free white craft glue

*cool idea*

*hinged-glass locket*

*pocket-watch locket*

## pocket-watch lockets

If needed, use the screwdriver to pry the back cover off of the locket. Cut a piece of paper the same size as the back cover and glue in place.

With the locket face down, fill with collage items, keeping in mind that the first items you add will be the most prominent; if your charms have loops, you may wish to cut them off using the wire cutters.

Press the back cover in place; if needed, lay the locket facedown on the terry-cloth towel, and use the hammer to gently tap the back into place.

## hinged-glass lockets

Unscrew the top of the locket by twisting the ball counter-clockwise. If filling with a card or paper, lay the locket over the image, trace around it with a pencil, and trim the paper about 1/8" (3 mm) inside the pencil line.

If filling with seeds or leaves, remember that the items will be slightly crushed when the locket is closed. Close the locket and secure by twisting the ball back down in the opposite direction.

**Note:** *Since both sides of the locket are glass, you may want to insert 2 pieces of paper back-to-back for a reversible pendant.*

vintage vogue

painted beauty

olympic medal

old world
emerald

**TOOLBOX**
Size 12 or 13 beading needle
Thread conditioner
Fabric-marking pen or pencil
Scissors

# cabochon craze

Ever find a favorite cabochon, button, or bead that you
know would look great encrusted with smaller beads? Here
you simply stitch into a felt backing to achieve the look of
intricately shaped, beadwoven cabochons.

## *vintage vogue*

### MATERIALS

25 gold size 15° charlottes

25 pale rose 3mm fire-polished rounds

1 sterling silver 15mm eye closure

1 black/gold 27mm vintage button

Double-sided craft tape or craft glue

2 x 2" (5 x 5 cm) piece of white
  Lacy's Stiff Stuff beading foundation

Pale rose nylon beading thread

1~ **PREPARATION.** If the button has a shank,
cut a small X in the center of the foundation to
accommodate for it. Center the button and trace
around the outside edge; set the button aside.

2~ **STITCHING.** Stitch along the outside
edge of the traced circle using fire-polished
rounds (the charlottes will be added during
a second pass):

**Pass 1:** Tie a double knot at the end of 24"
(61 cm) of thread and bring the needle up
$^{1}/_{16}$" (2 mm) outside the traced circle.

String 1 fire-polished round, slide the bead
down, and hold it in place against the foundation; take the needle to the back, inserting it
perpendicular to the fabric at the end of the
bead so that the stitch is the same length as
the bead {**Fig. 1**}. If the bead moves back and
forth, the stitch is too long; if the bead cannot
lie flat, the stitch is too short.

Bring the needle back up about $^{1}/_{16}$" (2 mm)
(or the size of the charlotte bead that will later
fill this space) away from the previous stitch,
string another fire-polished round, and stitch
it to the foundation as before. Repeat adding
beads around the circle.

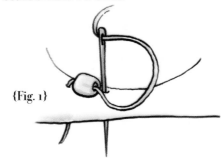

{Fig. 1}

**Pass 2:** Bring the needle up and pass through 1 fire-polished round. String 1 charlotte and pass through the next fire-polished round. Repeat around to add 1 charlotte between each fire-polished round {Fig. 2}. Pass through all beads again to reinforce.

{Fig. 2}

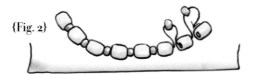

3~ **FINISHING.** Attach the button inside the ring of beads:

**Trim:** Carefully trim around the circle of beads to remove the excess foundation. If you accidentally cut a stitch, use needle and thread to pass through several beads near the cut stitch, following the same thread paths as before and angling the needle toward the center.

**Hanger:** Position the eye closure so that it overhangs the top of the pendant by about ¼" (6mm). Stitch it to the felt, passing through the small loops at the bottom of the eye closure.

**Adhere:** Coat the center of the foundation with glue or back the button with double-sided craft tape; press the button onto the foundation in the center of the bead ring.

If you cut an X during Step 1, use the needle and thread to stitch it up, passing under the shank of the button with each stitch. If desired, lightly coat the back with craft glue to help secure the threads.

*Note: If your button is thick and you wish for the beads to stay snug up against the button, cover the sides with double-sided craft tape and press the bead ring up around the side of the button.*

**Stringing:** For a suggestion on how to incorporate this pendant into a necklace, see the sidebar at far right.

**TIPS**

▶ *If you wish to conceal the stitches on the back the pendant, cut a circle or oval out of matching felt the size of the back of the pendant. Make a small slit in the back of the bail and glue in place.*

▶ *The eye closures used here as pendant hangers are actually part of a hook-and-eye clasp set. Use the eyes as bails and save the hooks for the projects on p.98 and 104.*

## old world emerald

{see pendant on p. 46 and at lower right}

### MATERIALS

13 white-lined olive green size 11° seed beads

13 olive green mottled 3mm fire-polished rounds

1 sterling silver 5x10mm decorative bail

1 green/silver 18mm vintage button

Double-sided craft tape or craft glue

2 x 2" (5 x 5 cm) piece of dark green wool felt

Green nylon beading thread

1~ **PREPARATION, STITCHING, AND FINISHING.** Repeat Steps 1–3 for the Vintage Vogue pendant, using the dark green felt and adding the fire-polished rounds in Pass 1 and the seed beads in Pass 2. To attach the bail, simply string the small loop at the bottom of the bail during one stitch of Pass 2. For a suggestion on how to incorporate this pendant into a necklace, see the sidebar at far right.

## olympic medal

### MATERIALS

34 teal matte size 11° seed beads

34 yellow matte 4x6mm teardrops

1 pale teal 36mm vintage pin, button, or cabochon

1 antique bronze 15mm eye closure

Double-sided craft tape or craft glue

3 x 3" (7.5 x 7.5 cm) piece of teal wool felt

Teal nylon beading thread

1~ **PREPARATION, STITCHING, AND FINISHING.** Repeat Steps 1–3 for the Vintage Vogue pendant using the teal felt and bronze eye closure. When working Pass 1, add seed beads and leave enough room between the beads to accommodate for the base of the teardrops. Add the teardrops in Pass 2.

## painted beauty

**MATERIALS**

24 white luster size 15° seed beads

23 silver-lined clear size 11° seed beads

24 light topaz 3mm fire-polished rounds

23 pale blue 4x6mm teardrops

1 black/gold/blue 18x24mm handpainted Russian flat oval bead or cabochon

1 sterling silver 5x13mm decorative bail

Double-sided craft tape or craft glue

2 x 2" (5 x 5 cm) piece of teal wool felt

Teal nylon beading thread

1~ **PREPARATION AND STITCHING.** This piece consists of 2 rings of beads. Repeat Step 1 for the Vintage Vogue pendant, using the teal felt.

**First bead ring:** Work 1 ring of beads as in Step 2 of the Vintage Vogue pendant: When working Pass 1, add the size 11° seed beads and leave enough room between the beads to accommodate for the base of the teardrops. Add the teardrops in Pass 2.

**Second bead ring:** Bead around the previous ring leaving only ⅛" (3 mm) between rings (the beads of the second ring will surround and prop up the teardrops of the first ring).

Repeat as in Step 2 of the Vintage Vogue pendant, adding the fire-polished rounds in Pass 1 and the size 15° seed beads in Pass 2.

2~ **FINISHING.** Attach the bail and oval bead:

**Bail:** Position the bail so that it overhangs the top of the pendant by about ¼" (6 mm). Stitch the bail to the felt, passing through the small loop at the bottom of the bail.

Make a few stitches that pass through the body of the bail to help secure it flat against the back of the felt.

**Adhere:** Repeat as in Step 3 of the Vintage Vogue pendant but in addition to gluing the bead in place, also pass through it several times to stitch it to the felt.

▲ *Attach a sterling silver 6mm jump ring to the top of the* **vintage vogue** *pendant and string with dusty purple 9×6mm glass rondelles, labradorite 4mm rounds, and bronze 3mm pressed-glass nuggets.*

## stringing *suggestions*

▼ *String the* **old world emerald** *pendant with green/amber mottled 7×5mm faceted pressed-glass rondelles, turquoise/black 4mm fire-polished rounds, and black/green mottled 4mm pressed-glass 3-sided rounds.*

# whimsical
# & weightless

These sweet and ornate pendants are a scrapbooker's delight. The finished texture and weightlessness of these embellished metal-rimmed tags are similar to shells, making them ideal for layering.

## *embossed pendants*

### MATERIALS

Paper and vellum metal-rimmed scrapbooking/office identification tags in metallic browns and grays

Metal-rimmed tags kit, decorative paper, and card stock for customized tags (optional)

Pigment- and dye-based ink pads in brick red, brown, pumpkin, sage green, and metallic silver

Embossing powder in clear, copper glitter, and pale mustard

Rubber stamps with natural motifs, abstract shapes, words, and ornamental patterns

5 sheets of white copier paper

1~ **WORK SURFACE.** Spread out 3 sheets of white paper and place a small pile of embossing powder on each sheet; do not mix colors.

2~ **STAMPING.** With the tag on one of the remaining sheets of paper, ink up a stamp, press it onto a tag, and before the ink dries, move the tag near one of the piles of embossing powder, and gently cover with the powder. Tap the tag to remove excess powder.

## ★ Tips

> ➤ *The tags used here are made of gray and tan paper and vellum. White tags from an office supply store may also be used.*
>
> ➤ *The pigment-based inks are thicker and drier and thus do not hold the embossing powder very well (which is great if a distressed look is desired); for crisp lines and bolder designs, use the dye-based ink.*

3~ **EMBOSSING.** Move the tag to the last sheet of paper. Turn on the heat tool and slowly move it back and forth a few inches away from the tag for several seconds (or as recommended by the manufacturer) until the powder is melted. Allow to cool. Leftover powder can be returned to the original containers.

4~ **EMBELLISHMENT.** Follow these guidelines when layering embellishments on the tags:

**Layering:** When using several layers of embossing powder, use caution not to heat the tag too quickly; heating slowly will keep you from accidently overheating the tag and melting the previous layers.

**Colors:** Remember that if you are using a dark embossing powder, like the copper glitter, the color of the ink doesn't matter as it will not show through the dark powder.

If you want the color of the ink to show, use the clear embossing powder. As a general rule, begin stamping with the lightest colors first as it is always easier to add dark layers on top of light.

**Edges:** To decorate just the edges of the tags, press the metal borders onto the edge of a stamp to wet with ink. Coat with embossing powder and heat as before.

5~ **CUSTOMIZED TAGS (OPTIONAL).** If using a kit to make your own tags, choose printed scrapbook papers for the center of the tags. Use the kit's template for cutting the paper, and then cut a duplicate piece out of card stock.

Before pinching the edges closed with flat-nose pliers, insert the piece of card stock behind the precut paper; this will help strengthen and stiffen the tag. Use the hole punch to form a hanging device.

6~ **FINISHING.** For suggestions on how to incorporate these pendants into a necklace, see the sidebar at right.

➤ Use 1 antique copper
9×12mm rectangle jump ring
to join 1 gray/burnt orange
23×26mm engraved teardrop
shell and 2 stamped and
embossed rectangles
(1 measuring 18×37mm and
the other 36×65mm). String
the pendant's jump ring with
pale blue seed beads, pineapple
quartz 6mm faceted rounds,
matte jasper 7mm rounds, and
matte gray marbled 12mm and
pale mint green 11mm vintage
Lucite rounds.

## stringing *suggestions*

➤ Use 1 antique copper 9mm
jump ring to join 1 gray/burnt
orange 20×40mm engraved
oval shell and 2 stamped and
embossed circles (1 mea-
suring 37mm and the
other 50mm). String
the pendant's jump
rings with topaz
3mm fire-polished
rounds, serpentine
7×5mm faceted
rondelles, matte moss
green marbled 11mm
vintage Lucite rounds, and
green/amber mottled 8mm
pressed-glass nuggets.

*links & rings*

*box clasp beauty*

*silver sequence*

*love bird*

TOOLBOX
Wire cutters
Round-nose pliers
Chain-nose pliers

# front & center

Have a treasured clasp that you just can't imagine hiding on the back of your neck? Design your focal piece around it. Plus, having the closure in front makes getting your necklace on and off a breeze.

## *links & rings*

### MATERIALS

9 smoky quartz 4x3mm faceted rondelles
12 silver 6mm faceted pressed-glass vintage nailhead coins
10 sterling silver 1½" (38mm) head pins
2 Thai silver 20mm links that match the clasp
1 Thai silver 20mm toggle clasp
4" (10 cm) of sterling silver 24-gauge wire

1~ **LINKS.** Use 2" (5 cm) of wire to form a wrapped loop that attaches to the ring half of the clasp; string 1 rondelle, 1 nailhead, and 1 rondelle. Form a wrapped loop that attaches to 1 link.

Use 2" (5 cm) of wire to form a wrapped loop that attaches to the other end of the previous link and string 1 rondelle, 1 nailhead, and 1 rondelle. Form a wrapped loop that attaches to the last link.

2~ **DANGLES.** Use a head pin to string 1 nailhead and 1 rondelle; form a wrapped loop that attaches to the top loop of the ring half of the clasp; repeat, omitting the rondelle. Repeat entire step to add 2 dangles to each top and bottom loop of the remaining links.

3~ **FINISHING.** For a suggestion on how to incorporate this pendant into a necklace, see the sidebar on p. 57.

## box clasp beauty

### MATERIALS

1 olivine 7x18mm faceted cubic zirconia teardrop

1 gold-filled 15x25mm box clasp with peridot inlay

4" (10 cm) of gold-filled 24-gauge wire

1~ **DANGLE.** Use the wire to string the teardrop and form a wrapped loop that attaches to the tab half of the clasp. Continue to wrap the tail down around the teardrop (see p. 36).

2~ **FINISHING.** Regardless of how you choose to finish the strands, the one that attaches to the tab half of the clasp should be longer, allowing the dangle to hang below the clasp. (In the sample shown here, 1x2mm oval chain was attached to the clasp loops using lark's head knots.)

## silver sequence

### MATERIALS

6 Thai silver 10–14mm irregular rings

1 Thai silver 23mm wrapped-wire toggle clasp

Diamond Glaze adhesive (optional)

24" (61 cm) of silver 26-gauge craft wire

1~ **RING CONNECTIONS.** Use wire to join the irregular rings and the clasp:

**Wrapped rings:** Use 8" (20.5 cm) of wire to string 4 rings, leaving a 1" (2.5 cm) tail; pass through them again and pull snug, making sure they will lie flat in stacks of 2 on your work surface.

Pass through the rings several more times. When about 1½" (3.8 cm) of wire remains, twist twice with the beginning tail, trim, and press flat against the wire loops (the side with the twists is the back of the pendant).

Repeat to join 2 more irregular rings to 2

of the previously joined rings. Use the same method to connect the last 2 rings to the ring half of the toggle clasp.

2~ **FINISHING.** If desired, place a small drop of Diamond Glaze on the twisted wire ends; this will help secure the ends and cover any sharp ends of the wire.

## love bird

{see pendant on p. 54 and at lower right}

### MATERIALS

1 turquoise mottled 5x9mm pressed-glass teardrop

2 pale green marbled 8x3mm pressed-glass flowers

1 kelly green 8mm vintage crystal vertically drilled flower

1 pale teal 10x14mm pressed-glass horizontally drilled oval

1 antique copper 16x18mm filigree charm

1 rose gold 25mm bird toggle clasp

1 antique copper 1" (25mm) head pin

7 antique copper 4mm jump rings

3 antique copper 6mm jump rings

¾" (2 cm) of antique copper 2x2–3mm long-and-short chain

1½" (3.8 cm) of brown 24-gauge craft wire

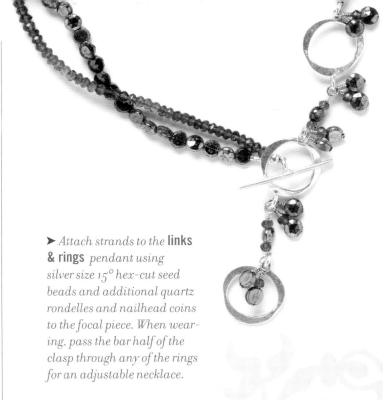

► *Attach strands to the* **links & rings** *pendant using silver size 15° hex-cut seed beads and additional quartz rondelles and nailhead coins to the focal piece. When wearing, pass the bar half of the clasp through any of the rings for an adjustable necklace.*

## stringing *suggestions*

▼ *Attach antique copper 5×7mm oval chain to the* **love bird** *pendant. Break the chain into sections using wrapped-loop links made of antique copper wire and erinite 8mm crystal rounds. Use antique copper 5mm jump rings to attach additional pale green marbled flowers to the links of the chain.*

1~ **DANGLES.** Make 4 dangles:

**Flowers:** Use a 6mm jump ring to string 1 pale green flower, attaching it to a 4mm jump ring. Use a second 4mm jump ring to attach the previous jump ring to the large loop of the ring half of the clasp.

Repeat for a second pale green flower, omitting one of the 4mm jump rings.

**Chain:** Use the head pin to string the kelly green flower and form a wrapped loop that attaches to one end of the chain. Use a 4mm jump ring to attach the other end of the chain to the large loop of the ring half of the clasp.

**Filigree and oval:** Join two 4mm jump rings to form a short chain. Use a 6mm jump ring to string the oval and attach it to the end of the jump-ring chain.

Use 1½" (3.8 cm) of wire to string the teardrop and form a wrapped-loop bail that connects to the bottom loop of the filigree charm.

Use one 4mm jump ring to join the free end of the jump-ring chain, the top of the filigree charm, and large loop of the ring half of the clasp.

2~ **FINISHING.** For a suggestion on how to incorporate this pendant into a necklace, see the sidebar at right.

*silver & stones*

*interchangeable charms*

*nature walk*

*take flight*

*mermaid's treasure*

*rectangle roundup*

TOOLBOX
Wire cutters
Round-nose pliers
Chain-nose pliers
Size 12 beading needle

# the more
# the merrier

Don't just use one favorite pendant—be an assembly artist.
Combine chains, dangles, and beads for a visually textured,
lyrical focal piece that is hard to keep your hands off of.

## *interchangeable charms*

### MATERIALS

1 burgundy 4mm crystal round

3 jonquil satin 4mm crystal bicones

1 pewter 26x10mm bird bead

1 fine silver 13mm fairy charm

1 sterling silver 17x15mm jack charm

1 fine silver 16x38mm helicopter seed charm

1 antique brass 6mm jump ring

1 antique brass 1½" (38mm) head pin

1 sterling silver 1½" (38mm) head pin

1 silver prefinished chain necklace

2" (5 cm) of brown 24-gauge craft wire

1~ **DANGLES.** Make 4 dangles, making sure that the loops of the dangles are large enough to fit over one end of the necklace's closure:
**Bird dangle:** Use the antique brass head pin to string 1 bicone, the bird bead, and 1 bicone; form a wrapped loop.
**Crystal dangle:** Use the sterling silver head pin to string the burgundy round and 1 bicone; form a wrapped loop.
**Fairy dangle:** Use the wire to string the fairy charm and form a wrapped-loop bail.
**Jack charm:** Attach the jump ring to the jack.

2~ **ASSEMBLY.** Use the necklace to string the bird dangle, seed charm, crystal dangle, fairy dangle, and jack charm.

## mermaid's treasure

### MATERIALS

10 green-lined amber AB size 11° seed beads

1 jade 6x10mm faceted teardrop

1 lemon quartz 10x14mm faceted briolette

1 pewter 8x23mm mermaid charm

1 seafoam green 22x25mm engraved shell teardrop pendant

1⅝" (4.2 cm) of sterling silver 2mm round chain

Pale green beading thread

4" (10 cm) of sterling silver 24-gauge wire

**1~ DANGLES.** Make 2 dangles:

**Jade teardrop:** Use 2" (5 cm) of wire to string the jade teardrop and form a wrapped-loop bail that attaches to one end of a ¾" (2 cm) piece of chain.

**Quartz briolette:** Repeat as for the jade teardrop, using the lemon quartz briolette and a ⅞" (2.2 cm) piece of chain.

**2~ ASSEMBLY.** Use 24" (61 cm) of thread to string the free end of the jade teardrop dangle chain, the mermaid charm, 1 seed bead, the free end of the quartz briolette dangle chain, the shell pendant, and 9 seed beads.

Pass through all beads and end chain links again to form a loop, leaving a 4" (10 cm) tail. Tie the tail and working thread into a knot and pass through the beads several more times to reinforce before knotting again and trimming the tails.

## take flight

{see pendant on p. 58 and at lower right}

### MATERIALS

1 bronze 4x7mm faceted pressed-glass tapered oval

1 antique brass 17x10mm bird charm

3 antique brass 3x4mm oval jump rings

1 antique brass 2mm earring finding with 2 loops

1 brass 17mm antique button with shank

1½" (38mm) antique brass 24-gauge wire

**1~ CHARM.** Join the oval jump rings to form a chain. Attach the last jump ring to the bird charm; attach the first to the lower loop of the earring finding.

**2~ BUTTON AND TEARDROP.** Use the wire to form a wrapped loop that attaches to the top loop of the earring finding; string the button shank and the oval. Form a wrapped loop to complete the link.

**3~ FINISHING.** For a suggestion on how to incorporate this pendant into a necklace, see the sidebar at right.

◄ To finish the **nature walk** pendant, fold a maroon 7mm ribbon in half and form a lark's head knot at the center of the 27mm ring; trim the ribbon ends at an angle to help prevent fraying (if the ribbon is made of synthetic materials, you can also melt the edges slightly with a lighter).

# nature walk

{see pendant on p. 58 and at right}

## MATERIALS

1 light topaz 8mm crystal bicone

1 dusty rose 4mm fire-polished round

1 fine silver 13mm fairy charm

1 fine silver 10x23mm leaf charm

1 fine silver 17x22mm oval tree charm

1 gray 18x20mm smooth stone pendant

10 brass 4mm jump rings

3 antique brass 9mm textured jump rings

1 gold-filled 27mm textured ring

1 brass/maroon 19mm ornate antique button with openwork/filigree

2 antique brass 1½" (38mm) head pins or 3" (7.5 cm) of dark brass 24-gauge wire

**1 ~ DANGLES.** Make 5 dangles:

**Leaf dangle:** Join four 4mm jump rings to form a chain. Attach the last jump ring to the leaf charm; attach the first jump ring to one 9mm jump ring.

**Stone dangle:** Attach one 9mm jump ring to the stone.

**Button dangle:** Cut the end off of a head pin (or use 1½" [3.8 cm] of wire) and form a wrapped loop that attaches to an opening in the button; string the fire-polished round. Form a wrapped loop that attaches to the 27mm ring to complete the link.

## stringing *suggestions*

◄ String the top wrapped loop of the **take flight** pendant with the following: matte moss green marbled 7mm vintage Lucite rounds, pale green 6mm fire-polished rounds, and cloudy gray and bronze 4mm fire-polished rounds.

**Tree dangle:** Join six 4mm jump rings to form a chain. Attach the last jump ring to the leaf charm; attach the first jump ring to one 9mm jump ring.

**Fairy dangle:** Cut the end off of a head pin (or use 1½" [3.8 cm] of wire) and form a simple loop that attaches to the fairy charm; string the bicone.

Form a simple loop that attaches to the 27mm ring, to the left of the button dangle, to complete the link.

**2~ ASSEMBLY.** Open the 9mm jump ring of the tree charm and attach it to the 27mm ring, between the fairy and button dangles.

Attach the stone and leaf dangles to the 27mm ring to the right of the button dangle, in that order.

**3~ FINISHING.** For a suggestion on how to incorporate this pendant into a necklace, see sidebar on p. 61.

## silver & stones

### MATERIALS

1 Fordite (made from layers of paint from a Ford automobile factory) or striped stone 11x18mm flat rectangle pendant

1 Fordite or striped stone 12x25mm tapered flat rectangle pendant

7 sterling silver 6mm jump rings

1 sterling silver 10mm triangle jump ring/bail

3 Thai silver 14mm detached chain links with decorative holes

**1~ DANGLES.** Make 2 dangles:

**Chain dangle:** Join the 6 jump rings to form a chain. Attach the last jump ring to the 11x18mm pendant.

**Rings dangle:** Use a jump ring to join 2 Thai silver rings, passing through the decorative holes.

**2~ ASSEMBLY.** Open the triangle bail/jump rings and string 1 Thai ring, passing through a decorative hole; slide the ring to the top of the bail to create the hanging device. String the free end of the chain dangle, one decorative hole of the rings dangle, and the 12x25mm pendant; close the triangle.

## rectangle roundup

### MATERIALS

1 burgundy 4mm crystal round

5 garnet 2.5mm rounds

3 copper 3mm rounds

1 fine silver 17x22mm decorative pendant

1 brown swirls 26x44mm ceramic pendant

3 copper 24-gauge 1" (25mm) head pins

12" (30.5 cm) of brown 28-gauge craft wire

**1~ DANGLES.** Use a head pin to string the crystal, 1 garnet round, 1 copper round, and 1 garnet round; form a simple loop.

Use a head pin to string 1 garnet round and 1 copper round; form a simple loop. Use a head pin to string 1 garnet round, 1 copper round, and 1 garnet round; form a simple loop.

**2~ ASSEMBLY.** Fold the brown craft wire in half and use the folded end to string all 3 dangles, the fine silver pendant, and the ceramic pendant.

Pass through the dangles and pendants again to form a ½" (1.3 cm) loop, leaving a 4" (10 cm) tail. Continue passing the wire through the dangles and pendants until 4" (10 cm) of wire remains.

Bend this tail, and the previous tail, to the top of the loop and wrap both around the top of the loop. Hide the wire tails in the loop and trim close.

## cool idea

# from vintage to vogue

Brooches and clip-on earrings can be used as pendants by simply using wire to create a bail or a commercially made brooch converter as a hanging device.

**TOOLBOX**

Wire cutters

Round-nose pliers

Flat-nose pliers

**MATERIALS**

Antique brooches or clip-on earrings

Silver and gold-filled 20–32mm brooch converters with vertical or horizontal tubes or 3" (7.5 cm) of 20-gauge wire

Assorted 3–6mm spacers

G-S Hypo Cement

## brooch pendants

**VERTICAL CONVERTER.** (Pin back will run parallel to bail.) Open the pin back and string a vertical converter and, if desired, enough spacers to cover the pin when closed.

For a permanent pendant, coat the spacers, top of the tube, and the pin's closure with cement to prevent it from flopping back and forth and accidentally opening.

**HORIZONTAL CONVERTER.** (Pin back will run perpendicular to bail.) Open the pin back, string 2 to 3 spacers, the horizontal converter, and 2 to 3 more spacers; if needed, adjust the number of spacers to center the converter on the back of the brooch. Coat with cement as above.

**BAIL.** If your brooch has an opening near the edge you may wish to skip the converter. Use 3" (7.5 cm) of wire to form a large wrapped-loop bail that includes the brooch.

## clip-on pendants

**VERTICAL CONVERTER.** Carefully remove part of the back of 1 earring below the hinge that allows the earring to open and close, using flat-nose pliers to break the hinge if needed (only a small hook will remain on the back of the earring).

Coat the end of the hook with cement and pass it through the tube of the vertical converter, from top to bottom. Apply more cement inside and around the tube to secure the earring in place.

*horizontal converter*

*vertical converter*

*back*

*front*

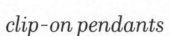

TOOLBOX

Tin snips

$1/_8$" (3mm) hole punch

Scissors

Wire cutters

Round-nose pliers

Flat-nose pliers

Gloves (cloth or thin leather)

# tiny tins

Quick, affordable, and cool, these tin boxes-turned-pendants will send you running for tin snips. Cut from new and vintage candy, watch, matchbook, spice, and coffee tins, they're a great way to recycle.

## tin pendants

### MATERIALS

New or vintage tin containers

Assorted copper, brass, and silver 7–12mm round and rectangle jump rings

$1/_{16}$–$1/_8$" (2–3mm) thick felt in colors to match tins

White acid-free craft glue

Super fine 400-grit sandpaper

Fine-line permanent marker

Assorted copper 20- and 24-gauge wire

1~ **CUTTING.** Choose an area on the tin to become a pendant and use the marker to outline the shape, using a ruler or tracing around objects like coins.

Don your gloves and carefully use the snips to cut inside the design line (wearing gloves will protect your hands from sharp edges). If cutting a shape with right angles, round the corners.

2~ **SANDING.** To smooth the edges of the tin, lay the sandpaper flat on your work surface and hold the tin face up at a 45° angle to the paper.

Drag the tin across the paper, smoothing any sharp edges; flip the tin and repeat on the other side. Hold the tin perpendicular to the paper and sand the edges again.

3~ **HOLES.** Use the hole punch to make 1 or 2 holes at the top of the pendant for hanging. Additional holes can be punched for design effects:

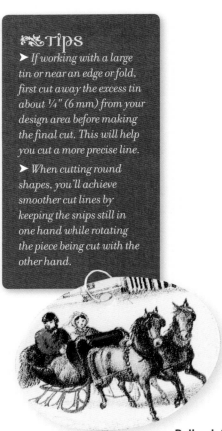

**Tips**

➤ If working with a large tin or near an edge or fold, first cut away the excess tin about ¼" (6 mm) from your design area before making the final cut. This will help you cut a more precise line.

➤ When cutting round shapes, you'll achieve smoother cut lines by keeping the snips still in one hand while rotating the piece being cut with the other hand.

**Polka dots:** For the look of polka dots, punch several holes at random in the pendant.

**Wrapped edges:** If you plan on wrapping the edge of the pendant (as seen on p. 64) in Step 5, turn the pendant over and use the marker to mark equally spaced holes; punch the holes.

4~ **FELT.** Cut a piece of felt that is about ¼–½" (6 mm–1.3 cm) larger than the pendant. Lightly coat the back of the pendant with glue, making sure not to allow the glue to pool in the pre-punched holes. Center the pendant over the felt and allow to dry.

Trim the felt, leaving ⅛" (3 mm) of felt around the pendant or trimming close to the edges, as desired.

If you wish, center the hole punch in the pre-punched holes and punch again to remove the felt.

5~ **HANGING.** Attach jump rings to the pendants or use wire to form hanging devices:

**Bail:** Using 5" (12.5 cm) of 20-gauge copper wire, string the top hole of a pendant and form a wrapped-loop bail.

**Wrapped edges and bail:** Use two 20" (51 cm) pieces of 24-gauge wire to string the top hole of the pendant from front to back. Pass both ends through the next hole, wrapping the wires around the edge of the pendant. Repeat around until you exit the top hole. Finish with a wrapped-loop bail.

6~ **FINISHING.** For a suggestion on how to incorporate these pendants into necklaces, see the sidebar at right.

◄ *This rectangular* **polka dot** *pendant was made from a tin that was purchased with a watch, and the felt behind the polka dots was left intact. Attach an antique copper 9×11mm rectangle jump ring, and string with moss green marbled 9mm vintage Lucite rounds, green speckled size 8° seed beads, and serpentine 4×3mm spacers.*

## stringing *suggestions*

▼ *This pendant was cut from an antique cookie tin printed with an advertisement for a Sears catalog. Attach an antique copper 8mm jump ring and string with teal 7mm vintage Lucite rounds and brown 10×4mm bone disc spacers.*

# charms

*Who doesn't love charms?* From supersweet and flowery to metallic and edgy, charms are enchanting finishing touches. Learn to create some of the most surprisingly simple charms out of unexpected, yet easy-to-find materials. The possibilities are endless: For a fun, musical bracelet (like the one on p. 70) that is sure to be noticed, string metal charms closely together and let them clang on your wrist like a tambourine. For your softer side, make charms out of fabric or wirework sweet little bead frames. You can even add a distinctly personal touch by suspending special pictures or tiny mementos inside a charm.

*silver chimes*

*open blossoms*

*flower buds*

*glamorous gold*

# charming caps & cones

Charms made of bead caps and cones strung closely together become a musical, rhythmic accessory. Using these common findings in a nontraditional way opens a multitude of creative opportunities.

## *silver chimes*

**MATERIALS**

White size 8° seed beads

Aqua 4x3mm faceted pressed-glass rondelles

Thai silver 7x14mm striped bead cones

Thai silver 13x18mm flared bead cones

Sterling silver 1½" (38mm) head pins

Use a head pin to string 1 seed bead, the wide end of 1 cone, and 1 rondelle; form a wrapped loop. Repeat for the desired number of dangles.

## *glamorous gold*

**MATERIALS**

Red and teal matte size 11° seed beads

Gold-filled 9x2mm hammered bead caps

Gold-filled 1" (25mm) head pins

Use a head pin to string the wide end of 1 bead cap and 1 seed bead; form a simple loop. Repeat for the desired number of dangles.

## *flower buds*

**MATERIALS**

Kelly green luster size 11° seed beads

Green with red-and-white spots 8mm glass rounds

Pewter 16x8mm flower bead caps

Sterling silver 1" (25mm) head pins

Use a head pin to string 1 spotted round, the wide end of 1 bead cap, and 1 seed bead; form a simple loop. Repeat for the desired number of dangles.

## *open blossoms*

**MATERIALS**

White and kelly green matte size 11° seed beads

Antique brass 7x3mm filigree flower bead caps

Antique brass 1½" (38mm) head pins

Use a head pin to string the wide end of 1 bead cap and 1 seed bead; form a wrapped loop. Repeat for the desired number of dangles.

**Tip**

*Be sure to close the simple loops tight to prevent the dangles from slipping off of your beading wire. For the most secure charm possible, finish your dangles with wrapped loops.*

# splash of pattern

Tones of romance, elegance, and subtle drama are easy to add using decorative rub-on transfers. The transferred image is essentially a thin, yet very durable sticker that is sealed with an acrylic spray.

## *patterned charms*

### MATERIALS

Assorted copper, brass, gold, and Thai silver 13–30mm diamond, oval, teardrop, pointed-oval, tabular, and round charms and small bezels

Black floral rub-on image transfers

Clear matte acrylic spray

1~ **PAPER.** The rub-ons consist of a backing paper (often waxy or made of tissue) that protects the images and the transfer paper that the sticker is temporarily adhered to. Without removing either of the papers, cut out the images you wish to transfer to your charms.

2~ **TRANSFERRING.** Wash and dry the charms/bezels. Remove the backing paper and lay the sticker face down on the charm (if using a bezel, lay the image on the back).

Rub the back of the transfer paper using the popsicle stick to transfer the sticker to the charm until you can see that the sticker is no longer attached to the paper (the paper often turns a lighter color when the sticker releases).

3~ **FINISHING.** To protect the stickers on the charm, lay the charms on a scrap piece of paper in a well-ventilated area and spray with several light coats of clear matte acrylic spray, waiting at least 2 minutes between coats, or according to manufacturer's directions.

**✳ TIP**
*If you have a hard time finding blank charms, use charms that are decorated on one side and transfer images to the other side.*

# soft & sweet

Soft, pliable fabric circles easily become durable, stringable charms with the use of a hole punch and an eyelet setter. Mix and match plain and patterned fabric scraps to coordinate with your most fashionable beads.

## soft charms

**MATERIALS**

Scraps of cotton fabric

Fusible web

$1/8$" (3mm) eyelets in colors to match fabrics

**1~ CUTTING.** Prepare the charms by cutting out the following materials:

**Fabric:** Use the fabric-marking pencil and circle template to draw ¾–1" (2–2.5 cm) circles on the fabric scraps; cut inside the line.

If working with thick fabric, one circle will yield one charm; if working with thin fabric (like quilter's cotton), cut 2 circles for each charm.

**Fusible web:** If working with 2 thin circles, cut out a circle of fusible web: To minimize fraying, cut circles of fusible web the same size as the circle; to encourage fraying, use the circle template to cut the circles of fusible web ¼" (6 mm) smaller than the fabric.

**2~ FUSING.** Preheat the iron. Lay the circle of fusible web face down on the wrong side of one circle of fabric. Following manufacturer's directions, iron the layers to fuse the web to the fabric.

Once cool, peel the paper backing off of the fusible web, place the second fabric circle on the first with wrong sides facing to sandwich the fusible web, and iron again to fuse the layers.

**3~ EYELETS.** Lay a fabric circle (or circle made of 2 fused layers) on the cutting mat or other protective surface.

**Punching:** Center the hole punch over the circle. Strike with the hammer several times to form a hole.

**Setting:** Insert 1 eyelet in the hole. Turn the charm over so that the tube end of the eyelet is facing up, center the eyelet setter over the eyelet, and strike with the hammer several times to set.

Repeat Steps 1 to 3 for the desired number of charms.

## ❋ what is fusible web?

*Fusible web is a nonwoven sheet of adhesive used to join two layers of fabric. The web comes temporarily adhered to a paper backing. It is laid facedown on the back of a fabric, the backing is ironed, then removed when cool. A second piece of fabric is placed over the web and the fabrics are ironed to fuse the layers. Web fuses more easily when the iron is very hot. Many synthetic fabrics will melt under heat so cotton fabrics are the easiest to fuse. Consider using a Teflon press cloth when ironing and make sure that the piece of web is always smaller than the fabric (otherwise you might accidentally fuse your project to your ironing board cover or dirty your iron).*

# charms mélange

Lovers of mixed media will delight in telling stories with charms embellished with maps, beads, and scrapbook papers. Seal these minicollages on bezels and blank charms for whimsical, sometimes funky accessories.

## *collage charms*

### MATERIALS

Assorted collage items: jump rings, decorative charms, antique watch parts, seed beads, crystal 2–4mm bicones, sequins, and filigree squares, circles, and wings

Scraps of decorative paper, including patterned scrapbook paper, paper with words, miniature tarot cards, stickers, and postage stamps (for backgrounds)

Brass, silver-plated, copper, and Thai silver 8–23x15–25mm blank diamond, oval, round, and pointed-oval charms

Assorted pewter, sterling silver, imitation rhodium, antique copper, and antique brass 24–30mm square, rectangle, round, and teardrop bezel settings

Epoxy, Amazing Glaze, and/or Diamond Glaze (see p. 78–80 for information when choosing a sealant)

Acid-free white craft glue

Polymer clay (optional)

Beading thread in colors to match seed beads (optional)

1 ~ **COLLAGE.** Prepare the charms and bezels for sealing:

**Background:** To determine the size of collage needed, trace around the charm or bezel on the background paper of your choice. Trim the paper, cutting $1/16$–$1/8$" (2–3 mm) inside the pencil line. Use a small amount of glue to adhere the background to the charm or bezel.

**Embellishments:** Cover the background with antique watch parts, filigree wings, seed beads, sequins, additional paper scraps, or papers with printed words. If layering papers, glue them together. If using lightweight items that move easily, glue them in place. If using deep bezels and Amazing Glaze, see p. 80 for tips for using polymer clay with decorative charms.

**Seed bead circle:** To create a circle of seed beads to line the bezels, use a needle and 18" (45.5 cm) of thread to string enough seed beads to fill the inside border of the bezel.

To test the size of the circle, hold the beads in a circle and place them inside the bezel. Once the

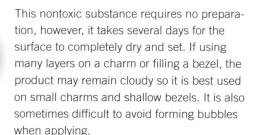

circle has enough seed beads to lie flat in the bezel, tie the ends together using a square knot and trim the ends. Return the circle to the bezel.

2~ **SEALING.** Choose from the three following products for sealing your collages inside the charms; it is important to choose the one that is best for your project. You will find additional materials and tools listed for use with each individual sealant.

### DIAMOND GLAZE
#### MATERIALS AND TOOLS
Scrap paper

Cotton swab or toothpick

Paintbrush (optional)

This nontoxic substance requires no preparation, however, it takes several days for the surface to completely dry and set. If using many layers on a charm or filling a bezel, the product may remain cloudy so it is best used on small charms and shallow bezels. It is also sometimes difficult to avoid forming bubbles when applying.

*Note:* *If your papers bleed when wet, they will bleed over time once sealed with Diamond Glaze. Light-colored paper can sometimes look transparent when wetted with the glaze.*

a~ Slowly coat the collage with Diamond Glaze; do not shake the bottle. If the glaze tends to bubble straight out the bottle, squeeze the first 1 to 2 drops on a scrap piece of paper before applying to the collage. If bubbles still exist, you can slide them off the side of the charm or bezel with a toothpick, or as the manufacturer suggests, break bubbles with a dry paintbrush (be sure to rinse the glaze off the paintbrush before it dries).

Excess glaze can be removed by rolling cotton swabs (if the tip of the swab is fuzzy, first smooth it by lightly wetting it with water to avoid leaving behind fibers in the glaze) or toothpicks into the surface immediately after applying it to the charm/bezel.

Allow to dry on a flat surface for several days. For a more domed effect, apply another thin coat but remember that using too many layers may result in a cloudy surface.

### EPOXY
#### MATERIALS AND TOOLS
2 small plastic cups and 2 wood stir sticks for mixing

Rubber or vinyl gloves

Wax or parchment paper

Plastic straw

Toothpicks

Epoxy dries quickly to a glasslike finish, is self-degassing so you never have to worry about bubbles, and sets up so hard that it can even be sanded. However, it is more toxic than Diamond Glaze, requires more preparation time, and must be mixed and poured in a well-ventilated area while wearing gloves.

*Note:* *Some epoxy brands require double-mixing, meaning that the two parts are first mixed in one container and then have to be mixed again in another clean container with a new stir stick.*

a~ Prepare a flat work surface with layers of waxed or parchment paper in a well-ventilated area; don your gloves. Mix the epoxy according to manufacturer's directions.

b~ To help transfer the epoxy from the mixing container to the charms/bezels, cut the tip of a straw at a 30° angle and use the tip as a scoop. If you happen to drizzle too much epoxy on a charm/bezel, quickly use a toothpick to drag or push the charm/bezel to a different area on the work surface, allowing the excess to run off the top edge.

c~ Continue to check the charms/bezels for the next hour or so, and if needed, drag or push them out of the puddle of excess epoxy with a toothpick.

## AMAZING GLAZE
### MATERIALS AND TOOLS

Baking tray

Parchment paper

Spoon or small scoop

Small paintbrush

Toothpicks

Polymer clay (optional)

Heat tool (optional)

Amazing Glaze comes as a powder, ready to be poured directly onto your charm/bezel. Since it must be baked in an oven, be sure that your collage is made only of materials that can withstand 275° F heat (paper burns at 451° F).

## ❋TIPS

➤ To ensure a smooth finish, do not choose collage items that are thicker than the bezel setting is deep—they will be difficult to completely coat with sealant.

➤ If working with a circular bezel that is difficult to trace around, measure the circle using a circle template. Then use the template to trace a same-size circle on the background paper.

*If you absolutely love making these charms, why not create a pendant using a larger 25–50mm bezel?*

*Simply follow the instructions for the collage charms to fill the bezels, then string with your most fabulous beads to create a trendy memento worn close to your heart.*

Choose papers that are light in color as the process of baking and sealing with resin powder will darken them. If you are using large collage items that are hollow on the back, the supplier suggests pressing a small amount of polymer clay into the back. This will prevent air from getting trapped under the charm and creating bubbles during baking. If you fill a deep bezel with a large amount of clay and bake the collage for too long, the polymer may float to the top, so it's a good idea to use a small amount of glue under the clay.

a~ Preheat oven to 275°F. Place the charm/bezel on a piece of parchment paper on your worktable and use the scoop or spoon to fill the bezel with resin powder, adding enough to form a dome on top.

b~ Carefully use the paintbrush to brush away any unwanted powder from the edges and transfer onto a parchment-lined baking tray (be sure not to spill any powder on an uncovered tray because once it is baked it is hard to remove). Pour any spilled powder back into the container.

c~ Carefully place the tray in the oven and bake according to manufacturer's directions (about 3 to 10 minutes), or until 30 to 45 seconds after all of the powder has melted. The thicker the bezel wall, the longer it will take to heat up and melt the powder, so if you are baking several bezels at once, make sure they are similar in size.

d~ Remove the tray from the oven and if no bubbles formed, allow to cool on an even surface for about 5 minutes. If bubbles form, quickly and carefully use a toothpick to pull the bubbles off the side of the charm/bezel or pick them up by rolling the toothpick into the glaze immediately after baking. You can also melt away small bubbles and smooth uneven surfaces with a heat tool by just heating the top surface of the charm/bezel (as opposed to re-baking the entire collage, which can cause the layers, especially those made of polymer clay, to shift). Do not attempt to melt additional powder to the top of the charm/bezel using the heat tool, the loose powder will be blown away by the tool's fan.

e~ If you would like the top of the charm/ bezel to be more domed, simply add more resin powder as before and bake again. You can repeat this process as many times as needed; however, if you filled a deep bezel with polymer clay, remember not to over-bake the pieces.

**Note:** *Be aware that collages are susceptible to cracking when exposed to extreme temperature changes. To avoid this, wear the collages close to your body during winter (your body heat will protect them). Should a crack accidently form, rebake the collages in the oven or reheat them with a heat tool to repair cracks.*

3~ **FINISHING.** For suggestions of how to incorporate these charms into necklaces and bracelets, see the sidebar at right.

◄ *Use antique copper and brass 4mm jump rings, gold size 15° seed beads, a bright brass 17×15mm bird charm, and teal scrapbook paper to create a collage inside an antique copper 18×30mm teardrop bezel setting. Seal with epoxy. Use an antique copper 6mm jump ring to attach the charm to antique brass 4×6mm oval chain; break the chain into sections using simple-loop links made of gunmetal 20-gauge craft wire, antique bronze 4mm cogged heishi washers, and rutilated quartz 8mm faceted rounds.*

## stringing *suggestions*

▼ *Embellish small silver and antique brass and copper charms with scrapbook paper and seal with Diamond Glaze. Attach 1 matching 6mm jump ring to the top of each charm. String the charms with rose 5mm vintage Lucite rounds, green with red-and-white spots 8mm glass rounds, and dusty rose 9×6mm glass rondelles.*

*charming hexagons*

*framed in gold*

*jeweled raindrops*

*free wheelin'*

*flirty links*

# bits & pieces

With just a few beads, head pins, and wire, small bead frames and detached chain links become dainty little charms. String them as a group or string them solo, either way these charms are a great use for all those extra beads in your stash.

## framed in gold
### MATERIALS
Teal and mottled black 4–5mm glass cubes
Gold 10mm square and round bead frames
Gold-filled 1" (25mm) head pins

Use a head pin to string one side of 1 bead frame, 1 cube, and the other side of the bead frame; make a simple loop to form a dangle. Repeat for the desired number of charms.

## flirty links
### MATERIALS
Assorted pink, purple, blue, and green 3–8mm fire-polished rounds, pressed-glass flowers, and vintage Lucite rounds
Thai silver 8mm printed detached chain links
Sterling silver 24-gauge wire

Use 1½" (3.8 cm) of wire to string 1 detached chain link and form a trapped-bead bail that includes 1–3 assorted beads. Repeat for the desired number of charms.

## charming hexagons
### MATERIALS
Assorted rose, bronze, turquoise, and light blue 3–5mm fire-polished rounds
Metal 7mm hexagonal bead frames
Sterling silver 1" (25mm) head pins

Use a head pin to string one side of 1 bead frame, 1 fire-polished round, and the other side of the bead frame; make a simple loop to form a dangle. Repeat for the desired number of charms.

## free wheelin'
### MATERIALS
Thai silver 14mm detached chain links with decorative holes
Sterling silver 6mm jump rings

Attach a jump ring to one of the decorative holes in 1 of the detached chain links. Repeat for the desired number of charms.

## jeweled raindrops
### MATERIALS
Olivine, Pacific opal, tourmaline, chrysolite, smoked topaz, and khaki 3mm and 4mm crystal bicones
Brushed silver 10x14mm teardrop bead frames
Sterling silver 1" (25mm) head pins

Use a head pin to string one 3mm bicone and one side of 1 bead frame, from the inside out. String one 4mm bicone and make a simple loop to form a dangle. Repeat for the desired number of charms, omitting the inside 3mm bicone, if desired.

# CLaSPS 3

*Clasps can make or break a design,*
even if you string the most beautiful beads
imaginable. Whether your closure blends
in with the beads of your beautiful accessory, like the wireworked hook-and-eye
clasps, or make a statement of their own,
like the dangle-encrusted chain, the
handmade clasps that follow are winning
ways to end a project. Dress it up, add
some pizzazz, make it unique—you'll never
again think of a clasp in the same way.

*ring of citrine*

*ring-o-honey*

*labradorite blues*

*rubies-go-round*

TOOLBOX

G-S Hypo Cement

Scissors

Size 10 and 12 beading needles

Wire cutters

Round-nose pliers

Chain-nose pliers

# beaded ring toggles

Simple brick stitch makes bead frames beautiful. Don't be dismayed if you've never tried this stitch before, it is surprisingly quick and easy. You'll want to wear your hair up to show off these unique and easily customizable clasps.

## *labradorite blues*

### MATERIALS

10 blue 3mm fire-polished rounds

38 labradorite 4mm rounds

1 navy 35mm vintage Lucite ring

1 imitation rhodium 3" (75mm) head pin

Light blue/aqua permanent marker

K.O. white 100% polyester beading thread

5½" (14 cm) of sterling silver 20-gauge wire

**1~ RING EMBELLISHMENT.** Color 6' (1.8 m) of beading thread with the permanent marker and allow to dry. Use the beading thread and the size 10 needle to attach rounds to the outside edge of the bead frame:

**Beads 1 and 2:** Pass through the frame and tie a square knot on the outside of the ring. Glue the knot and allow to dry.

String 2 beads, pass through the frame, and pass back through the second bead strung; pull snug {Fig. 1}.

**Note:** *You may find it helpful to hold the ring in your nondominant hand; position the beads along the outside of the frame and hold them between your index finger and thumb as you pass back through the second bead.*

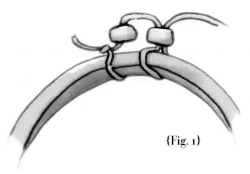

{Fig. 1}

**Bead 3:** String 1 bead, pass through the frame, and pass back through the bead just strung; pull snug **{Fig. 2}**.

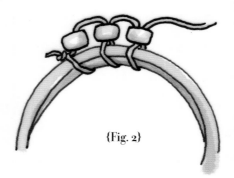

{Fig. 2}

**Beads 4 and on:** Repeat around as for Bead 3 until the frame is surrounded. Pass up through Bead 1. Switch to the size 12 needle if you find it hard to pass the needle and thread through the bead a second time.

To secure, pass through all beads again, following the previously stitched path. Tie a knot before trimming the thread; glue the knot.

**2~ RING BAIL.** Grip 3" (7.5 cm) of wire with the flat-nose pliers, 1" (2.5 cm) from one end of the wire and fold it down over the pliers to form a U shape.

String the embellished ring, positioning it in the U of the wire. Use the short end to wrap the base of the long wire, just above the beads. Use the long end to string 1 fire-polished round, 1 labradorite round, and 1 fire-polished round; form a wrapped loop (this completes a wrapped-loop link with bail).

**3~ BAR HALF.** Form the bar half of the clasp using a head pin and wire:
**Link:** Use 2" (5 cm) of wire to form a wrapped loop; string 1 fire-polished round, 1 labradorite round, and 1 fire-polished round. Form a wrapped loop to complete the link.

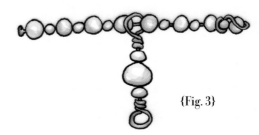

{Fig. 3}

**Head pin:** Use the head pin to string {1 labradorite round and 1 fire-polished round} three times. String 1 labradorite round, one end of the previously formed link, and 1 labradorite round. String {1 fire-polished round and 1 labradorite round} three times.

Push the beads down the base of the head pin, bend the head pin just above the last bead strung, and wrap the tail around the head pin between the last 2 beads **{Fig. 3}**.

## ring-o-honey
### MATERIALS
26 honey opal 4mm rounds

1 antique brass 32mm filigree ring

1 natural brass 5x41mm twig

Smoke FireLine 6 lb beading thread

4" (10 cm) of gunmetal 20-gauge craft wire

**1~ RING HALF.** Use the honey opal rounds and 6' (1.8 m) of FireLine to embellish the filigree ring as for the Labradorite Blues ring.

**2~ BAR HALF.** Leaving a 2" (5 cm) tail, tightly wrap the wire around the center of the twig (if the twig you are using has a hole in the center, pass through the hole on one of the passes).

Complete the bail by wrapping the tail around the base of the long wire two to three times (on the back of the twig); trim. Form a wrapped loop with the remaining wire.

## *rubies-go-round*

**MATERIALS**

8 ruby satin 4mm crystal bicones

4 light topaz 4mm fire-polished rounds

25 garnet 4mm rounds

1 dark wood 28mm bead frame

2 gunmetal 2" (50mm) head pins

Smoke FireLine 6 lb beading thread

1~ **RING EMBELLISHMENT.** Use the garnet rounds and 6' (1.8 m) of FireLine to embellish the wood bead frame as for the Labradorite Blues ring.

2~ **RING CONNECTION.** Use 1 head pin to string one hole of the bead frame, from the inside out; form a wrapped loop.

3~ **BAR HALF.** Use 1 head pin to string 1 bicone. String {1 fire-polished round and 2 bicones} three times. String 1 fire-polished round and 1 bicone. Finish the tail of the head pin as for the Labradorite Blues clasp.

## *ring of citrine*

**MATERIALS**

29 citrine 3mm rounds

1 brown 30mm mother-of-pearl bead frame

1 natural brass 5x41mm twig

1 copper 1½" (38mm) head pin

Orange/red permanent marker

K.O. white 100% polyester beading thread

4" (10 cm) of copper 20-gauge craft wire

1~ **RING HALF.** Color 6' (1.8 m) of beading thread with the permanent marker and allow to dry. Use the citrine rounds to embellish the mother-of-pearl bead frame as for the Labradorite Blues ring.

2~ **RING CONNECTION.** Use 1 head pin to string one hole of the bead frame, from the inside out; form a wrapped loop.

3~ **BAR HALF.** Use the copper wire to wrap the twig and form a bail as for the Ring-O-Honey clasp.

*golden links*

*brilliant brass*

*gunmetal glam*

*silver blossoms*

# charmed chains

Now the back of your necklace is as beautiful and eye-catching as the front. We've all seen adjustable necklaces finished with a plain and simple extender chain, but why not decorate the links with dangles? Don't dare let a link go unadorned.

## *golden links*

### MATERIALS

8 ruby satin 4mm crystal bicones

4 Pacific opal 4mm crystal bicones

1 amber mottled 5x3mm pressed-glass rondelle

1 German gold 7x12mm lobster clasp

4 gold-filled 1½" (38mm) head pins

3½" (9 cm) gold-filled 2–3x2–7mm long-and-short oval and round chain

9" (23 cm) of gold-filled 24-gauge wire

1~ **LINKS.** Cut the chain into 7 sections so that each oval link has a round link on each end.

*Use 1½" (3.8 cm) of wire to form a wrapped loop that attaches to the end of one section; string 1 ruby satin bicone. Form a wrapped loop that attaches to one end of another section of chain.

Repeat from * four times, connecting sections of chain with wrapped-loop links and alternating between Pacific opal and ruby satin bicones.

2~ **DANGLES.** Use a head pin to string 1 Pacific opal; form a wrapped loop that attaches to the round link on the end of the first section of chain.

Repeat to form 1 ruby satin dangle, 1 ruby satin and Pacific opal dangle, and 1 dangle that includes the following: 1 ruby satin, 1 rondelle, and 1 ruby satin. Attach these 3 dangles to the oval link of the first section of chain.

3~ **FINISHING.** Form a wrapped-loop link that includes a ruby satin bicone and join the remaining section of chain to the clasp.

## gunmetal glam

**MATERIALS**

15 black/green mottled 4mm pressed-glass 3-sided rounds

37 aquamarine 5x3mm faceted rondelles

1 sterling silver 16x22mm hammered clasp hook

27 gunmetal 2" (50mm) head pins

3½" (9 cm) of gunmetal 7mm rollo chain

1~ **DANGLES.** Use a head pin to string 2 aquamarine rondelles and form a simple loop that attaches to the first link of the chain; repeat for a second simple-loop dangle that also attaches to the first link.

Make a simple-loop dangle with the following combination of beads, attaching it to the first link of chain: one 3-sided round, 1 aquamarine rondelle, and one 3-sided round. Repeat to form a simple-loop dangle with one 3-sided round and 1 aquamarine rondelle that attaches to the first link.

Use a head pin to string 1 aquamarine and form a simple loop that attaches to a previously formed dangle; repeat for a second aquamarine/simple-loop dangle.

Repeat entire step to form matching clusters of dangles at the seventh, thirteenth, and nineteenth links of chain.

2~ **HOOK.** Make simple-loop dangles with the following combination of beads, attaching each to the hook: one 3-sided round, 1 aquamarine rondelle, and one 3-sided round; 1 aquamarine rondelle, one 3-sided round, and 1 aquamarine rondelle; and 2 aquamarine rondelles.

## brilliant brass

**MATERIALS**

5 antique rose 8mm faceted crystal rounds

5 prairie green 6x10mm faceted pressed-glass tapered ovals

2 natural brass 5x20mm printed charms

10 natural brass 8x3mm decorative bead caps

1 natural brass 8x12mm lobster clasp

10 natural brass 1½" (38mm) head pins

2 natural brass 5mm jump rings

4" (10 cm) of natural brass 10mm round chain

1~ **DANGLES.** Use a head pin to string 1 crystal round and 1 bead cap (wide end first); form a wrapped loop that attaches to the first link of the chain. Repeat using 1 oval and 1 bead cap for a second wrapped-loop dangle.

\*Use a head pin to string 1 crystal round and 1 bead cap; form a wrapped loop that attaches to the next chain link. Repeat from \* to attach one wrapped-loop dangle to each of the next seven chain links, alternating between crystals, rounds, and ovals.

2~ **CHARMS.** Use jump rings to attach 1 charm between the dangles on the first chain link and to the seventh link.

**Tip**

*If you add so many dangles that the chain becomes heavy, you'll need to use a heavy pendant to counterbalance the weight of the chain. Otherwise the necklace will want to slide down your back.*

## silver blossoms

### MATERIALS

4 cantaloupe 8mm faceted crystal rounds

3 erinite 8mm faceted crystal rounds

10 Thai silver 8x4mm flower bead caps

1 sterling silver 10x12mm lobster clasp

4 sterling silver 1½" (38mm) head pins

3 sterling silver 5mm jump rings

5" (12.5 cm) of sterling silver 10mm round chain

1½" (3.8 cm) of sterling silver 13x20mm oval chain

7½" (19 cm) of sterling silver 24-gauge wire

1~ **CHAIN.** Cut the 10mm chain into six 3-ring sections. If needed, cut the 13x20mm oval chain so that there are only two links of chain.

2~ **LINKS.** Join segments of chain using links:
**First link:** Use 2½" (6.5 cm) of wire to form a double-wrapped loop (if you only wrap once, the bead cap may not stay in place because of its large hole); string 1 bead cap (narrow end first), 1 cantaloupe crystal, 1 bead cap (wide end first), and form a double-wrapped loop that attaches to two 3-link sections of 10mm chain.
**Second link:** Repeat as for the first link using 1 erinite crystal to form a link that connects the free ends of the previous 10mm chains to 1 link of the 13x20mm oval chain.
**Third link:** Repeat as for the first link using 1 cantaloupe crystal and connecting the free end of the 13x20mm oval chain to 2 new 3-ring sections of 10mm chain.

3~ **DANGLES.** Make 4 dangles:
**Erinite:** Use a head pin to string 1 erinte crystal and 1 bead cap (wide end first); form a double-wrapped loop that attaches to the free ends of the previous 10mm chains.

Repeat to form a second erinite dangle; use a jump ring to attach the dangle to one 13x20mm oval chain link.
**Cantaloupe:** Use a head pin to string 1 cantaloupe crystal and 1 bead cap; form a double-wrapped loop. Repeat for a second cantaloupe dangle.

Use a jump ring to attach 1 cantaloupe dangle to the 10mm chain rings just below the first cantaloupe link. Use a jump ring to attach the second dangle just below the second cantaloupe link.

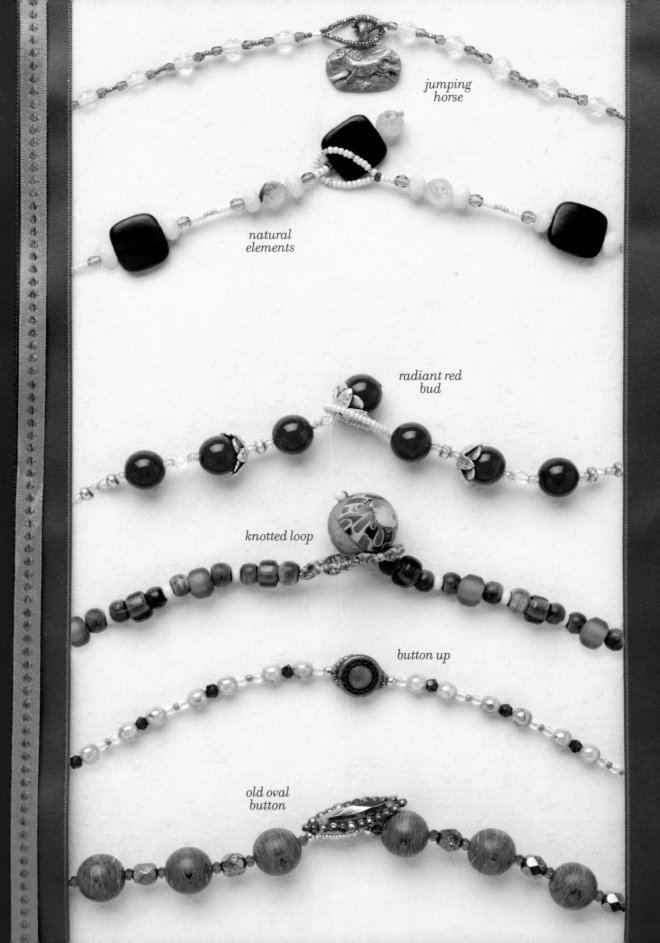

*jumping horse*

*natural elements*

*radiant red bud*

knotted loop

button up

*old oval button*

# lasso loops

Lasso a favorite large bead, charm, or button with a loop made of seed beads or knotted cord for a simple-to-make clasp. Made of the same beads in your project, this is the most affordable way to finish and coordinate your clasp with your design.

## old oval button

**MATERIALS**

About 50 gold size 15° charlottes

1 gray 12x32mm oval vintage button with shank

2 gold-filled 2mm crimp tubes

2 gold-filled 3mm crimp covers

Gray .019 beading wire

1~ **LOOP.** Use the wire to string 1 crimp tube and about 40 charlottes; pass back through the tube but do not crimp. Test the loop over the button, adjust the number of charlottes if necessary and crimp the crimp tube. Cover the crimp tube with a crimp cover.

2~ **BUTTON.** After stringing your necklace or bracelet, string 1 crimp tube, about 7 char-lottes, and the shank of the button. Pass the wire back through the crimp tube and snug the beads so that the charlottes cover the wire that passes through the shank; crimp and cover the crimp tube with a crimp cover.

## natural elements

**MATERIALS**

About 7 gold size 15° charlottes

About 25 pearly white size 11° seed beads

1 rutilated quartz 8mm faceted round

1 dark brown 16mm wood flat square bead

2 brass 2mm crimp beads

Gray .019 beading wire

1~ **STOP BEAD.** Use one end of the wire to string 1 crimp bead, the flat square bead, the rutilated quartz round, and 1 charlotte. Pass back through the rutilated quartz, flat square bead, and 1 crimp bead. Snug the beads and flatten the crimp bead.

2~ **LOOP.** After stringing your necklace or bracelet, use the other end of the wire to string 1 crimp bead and a mix of about 25 pearly white seed beads and 6 charlottes; pass back through the crimp bead but do not crimp. Before crimp-ing, test the length of the loop as for the Old Oval Button clasp, then flatten the crimp bead.

## jumping horse

{see clasp on p. 94}

**MATERIALS**

About 60 amethyst size 15° charlottes

1 pewter 22x20mm horse charm with large loop

3 sterling silver 1x2mm crimp tubes

Gray .014 beading wire

1 ~ **LOOP.** Use the wire to string 2 crimp tubes and about 45 charlottes; pass back through the tubes but do not crimp. Before crimping, test the length of the loop as for the Old Oval Button clasp, then flatten the crimp tubes.

2 ~ **CHARM.** After stringing your necklace or bracelet, string 1 crimp tube, about 15 charlottes, and the loop of the charm. Pass the wire back through the crimp tube and snug the beads so that the charlottes cover the wire as it passes through the loop; flatten the crimp tube.

## button up

{see clasp on p. 94}

**MATERIALS**

About 35 teal speckled size 11° seed beads

1 bronze 13mm round vintage button with shank

2 gold-filled 2mm crimp tubes

2 gold-filled 3mm crimp covers

Gold-colored .019 beading wire

1 ~ **LOOP.** Use the wire to string 1 crimp tube and about 25 seed beads; pass back through the tube but do not crimp. Before crimping, test the length of the loop as for the Old Oval Button clasp, then crimp the crimp tube. Cover the crimp tube with a crimp cover.

2 ~ **BUTTON.** After stringing your necklace or bracelet, string 1 crimp tube, about 10 seed beads, and the shank of the button. Pass the wire back through the crimp tube and snug the beads so that they cover the wire as it passes through the loop; crimp and cover the crimp tube with a crimp cover.

## radiant red bud

{see clasp on p. 94 and at lower right}

**MATERIALS**

About 40 pearly light blue size 11° seed beads

1 cranberry marbled 12mm vintage Lucite round

1 Thai silver 13x5mm bead cap

1 sterling silver 2" (50mm) head pin

2 brass 2mm crimp tubes

Silver-plated .019 beading wire

1 ~ **DANGLE.** Use the head pin to string the Lucite round and 1 bead cap (wide end first); form a wrapped loop. Use the wire to string 1 crimp tube, 2 seed beads, the wrapped loop, and 2 seed beads; pass the wire back through the crimp tube, snug the beads, and crimp.

2 ~ **LOOP.** After stringing your necklace or bracelet, use the other end of the wire to string 1 crimp tube and about 35 pearly light blue seed beads; pass back through the crimp tube but do not crimp. Before crimping, test the length of the loop as for the Old Oval Button clasp, then crimp the crimp tube.

3 ~ **FINISHING.** For a suggestion on how to incorporate this clasp into a necklace or bracelet, see the sidebar at far right.

## knotted loop

{see clasp on p. 94 and at top right}

**MATERIALS**

2 cream size 8° seed beads

1 tan/green/gray 18mm polymer clay round

1 safety pin

Thread burner, match, or lighter

Green and tan nylon beading cord

1 ~ **LOOP.** Take 1 strand of green cord and 1 strand of tan cord and fold them in half. Form a small loop by using both as 1 cord to tie an overhand knot near the end of the fold.

Use the safety pin to secure the small loop to

---

### ✿ Tips

➤ *When making seed bead loops, add 1 or 2 more seed beads than you think are needed; the wire loop will tighten when the tube is crimped.*

➤ *Choose the size of beading wire that is best for your design; the size used here is merely a suggestion. See p. 137 for tips on choosing crimp tubes and beading wire.*

➤ *Test the size of the loop by sliding it over the button; if the loop is too snug, it may weaken over time due to the stress of forcing the button through; if it is too large, the button may slip through accidentally. Adjust the length as necessary.*

a pillow. Hold 1 tan cord and 1 green cord taut in your nondominant hand, pulling toward you and away from the pillow. Use the other 2 cords to form half-hitch knots over the first 2 cords {Fig. 1}.

Continue knotting for about 2¾" (7 cm) {Fig. 2}, or until you have created a knotted cord long enough to form a loop that fits over the polymer bead. To test its length, form a large loop by passing 2 of the cord ends through the small loop; if needed, undo the loop and make more knots.

Once the correct size is achieved, pass 2 cord ends through the small loop, tie all cords together, trim the tails, and lightly melt the ends.

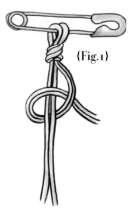

{Fig.1}

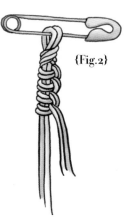

{Fig.2}

2~ **STOP BEAD.** After string-ing/knotting your necklace or bracelet, use 1 strand of green cord and 1 strand of tan cord to string 1 seed bead, the polymer round, and 1 seed bead.

Pass both ends back through the polymer round and first seed bead strung. Use an overhand knot to tie the cords together. Trim the tails and melt the ends.

3~ **FINISHING.** For a suggestion on how to incorporate this clasp into a necklace or bracelet, see the sidebar at right.

> ➤ *Pair the beads of the* **knotted loop** *clasp with wood 6–8×6mm rondelles, teal shiny and matte 9×6mm glass rondelles, and more size 8° seed beads.* **Note:** *Choose rondelles with large holes and string them close to the clasp so that they cover the cord knots.*

## stringing *suggestions*

> ▼ *Pair the beads of the* **radiant red bud** *clasp with Thai silver 5×2mm spacers, light blue 3mm fire-polished rounds, clear 4mm fire-polished rounds, and additional cranberry Lucite rounds and Thai silver bead caps.*

simple stones

SA Switzerland

plain
jane

sweet
spots

filigree fun

best boro

**TOOLBOX**
Wire cutters
Flat-nose pliers
Round-nose pliers
Ballpoint pen
Bench block
Ball-peen hammer

# beady hooks & eyes

Why break the sequence of your beautifully strung beads with an overbearing closure? Make your own out of wire using matching beads. Warm up by making hammered hook-and-eye clasps, then advance to incorporating beads into the links.

## *plain jane*

**MATERIALS**
5¼" (13.5 cm) of sterling silver 14-gauge dead-soft wire
5¼" (13.5 cm) of gold-filled 16-gauge dead-soft wire
Liver of sulfur (optional)

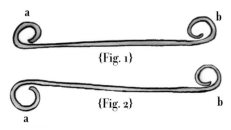

{Fig. 1}

{Fig. 2}

1~ **HOOKS.** Hammer the ends of 2¾" (7 cm) of sterling silver wire and 2¾" (7 cm) of gold-filled wire. First curl the ends, then follow the instructions below to finish them into hooks:

**Top curl:** Grip one flat end of one wire with the round-nose pliers and curl the tail toward the center just until it touches the wire, as if making a simple loop {Fig. 1a}. Repeat using the gold wire and position the wire so the loop points down {Fig. 2a}.

**Bottom curl silver hook:** Curl the other end of the silver wire, curling the wire toward the center in the same direction as the top curl and exaggerating the amount of curl to create a larger bottom loop {Fig. 1b}; you will attach the strand to this loop.

**Bottom curl gold hook:** Curl the other end of the gold wire, curling the wire toward the center in the opposite direction as the first curl and exaggerating the curl as before {Fig. 2b}.

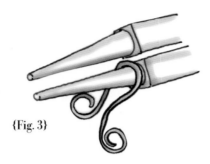

{Fig. 3}

**Shaping silver hook:** Use the largest part of the round-nose pliers to shape the center of the clasp into a hook:

Grip the silver wire about ½" (1.3 cm) from the top curl and with the curls pointing up, bend the wire down over the pliers {Fig. 3}.

Continue bending the wire and moving the pliers until the desired shape is achieved.

**Shaping gold hook:** Repeat shaping for the gold wire; the top curl will curl to the inside of the hook and the bottom curl will curl to the outside of the hook {Fig. 4}.

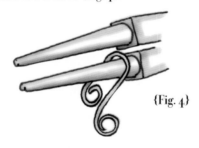

{Fig. 4}

2~ **EYES.** Wrap the end of 2½" (6.5 cm) of wire (gold or silver to match the hooks) around the center of the ball-point pen.

After one full loop, remove the wire and use the flat-nose pliers to grip the sides of the wire. Use your hand to continue curling the wire, adjusting the pliers as necessary to form a tight spiral {Fig. 5}. Trim the wire end at a 45° angle away from the curls.

{Fig. 5}

3~ **HAMMERING AND FINISHING.** Flatten the hooks and eyes using the flat end of the hammer; if desired, hammer only the large curve of the hooks.

Hammer again with the ball-peen end for a decorative look. If desired, oxidize the silver hook-and-eye set using liver of sulfur (see p. 103).

## sweet spots

### MATERIALS

2 dusty purple 9x6mm lampworked glass rondelles

1 mustard/pink spotted 16x10mm lampworked glass rondelle

4¾" (12 cm) of gold-filled 16-gauge dead-soft wire

1~ **HOOK.** Use 1¾" (4.5 cm) of wire to form a hook, following the directions for the Plain Jane silver hook.

2~ **EYE WITH SIMPLE-LOOP LINK.** Use 3½" (9 cm) of wire to form a large (¼–½" [6 mm–1.3 cm]) simple loop.

String 1 dusty purple rondelle, the mustard/pink spotted rondelle, and 1 dusty purple rondelle; form a simple loop about half the size of the previously formed loop.

3~ **HAMMERING.** Lay the simple loops on the side of the bench block so that the beads of the link hang off the edge. Hammer the simple loops, making sure not to strike the beads.

## best boro

**MATERIALS**

2 Montana blue 5mm crystal rounds

1 amber/teal/cream 13x8mm lampworked borosilicate rondelle

7" (18 cm) of gold-filled 20-gauge half-hard wire

1~ **HOOK.** Use 2" (5 cm) of wire to form a hook, following the directions for the Plain Jane gold hook.

2~ **EYE WITH WRAPPED-LOOP LINK.** Use 5" (12.5 cm) of wire to form a large (¼–½" [6 mm–1.3 cm]) wrapped loop. String 1 crystal round, the lampworked rondelle, and 1 crystal round; form a wrapped loop about half the size of the previously formed loop.

3~ **HAMMERING.** Finish as for the Sweet Spots clasp.

## simple stones

**MATERIALS**

2 aquamarine 5x3mm faceted rondelles

1 serpentine 7x5mm faceted rondelle

1 sterling silver ½ x ¾" (1.3 x 2 cm) clasp hook

2½" (6.5 cm) of sterling silver 20-gauge dead-soft wire

1~ **EYE WITH WRAPPED-LOOP LINK.** Use 2½" (6.5 cm) of wire to form a large (¼–½" [6 mm–1.3 cm]) wrapped loop.
  String 1 aquamarine rondelle, the

serpentine rondelle, and 1 aquamarine rondelle; form a wrapped loop about half the size of the previously formed loop.

2~ **HAMMERING.** Finish as for the Sweet Spots clasp.

## filigree fun

**MATERIALS**

3 chrysolite satin 6mm crystal rounds

1 antique brass 15mm filigree round

9½" (24 cm) of gunmetal 20-gauge half-hard craft wire

1~ **HOOK WITH WRAPPED LOOP.** Use 4½" (11.5 cm) of wire to form the top curl of a hook, following the directions for the Plain Jane gold hook but instead of forming the bottom curl, bend the wire up at a 90° angle, string one 6mm round, and form a wrapped loop.

2~ **EYE WITH WRAPPED-LOOP LINK.** Use 5" (12.5 cm) of wire to form a large (¼–½" [6 mm–1.3 cm]) wrapped loop.
  String 1 crystal round, the filigree round, and 1 crystal round; form a wrapped loop about half the size of the previously formed loop.

3~ **HAMMERING.** Finish as for the Sweet Spots clasp. **Note:** *Because craft wire tends to be soft, hammer lightly.*

# distress it

Whack it, file it, bend it, even change the color of it with a hard-boiled egg! Be amazed by how fun it is to transform an average clasp into something unique.

## TOOLBOX

Hammers (jeweler's and household)

Bench block

File

Safety glasses

## MATERIALS

Assorted Thai silver, gold-filled, copper, brass, and sterling silver toggle clasps, S-clasps, and hooks

Black patina

Liver of sulfur

220-grit sandpaper or coarser

Rubber or vinyl gloves

Disposable plastic or glass containers, at least one airtight

Baking soda

Polishing cloth and/or #0000 steel wool

Sewing thread

Egg and stove, pan, and water for boiling

Tape

## *distressing*

1~ **TEXTURE.** Alter the surface texture of a clasp with one or more of the following methods:

**Hammer:** Hammer the edges of a clasp for an asymmetrical look. For a highly textured surface, don your safety glasses, lay the closure on a concrete surface, and hammer (you should not use your good jeweler's hammer for this); for a smoother surface, use the bench block and your jeweler's hammer.

**Sand and file:** Roughen the surface with files and sandpaper for a matte finish.

2~ **COLOR.** When chemically altering the color of metal, always wear gloves, work in a well-ventilated area (liver of sulfur has an unpleasant odor and dangerous fumes), and carefully read manufacturer's directions.

   Wash all clasps with soap and water and use 12" (30.5 cm) of thread to string one half of the clasp and use the ends to tie an overhand knot. Use one of the following methods to alter color:

**Patina:** Pour a small amount of patina into a disposable container. For allover color, dip the entire piece into the patina.

For stripes, slowly lower the piece partially into the liquid and hold the piece still. Once desired color is achieved, rinse the pieces in cold water.

**Liver of sulfur:** Unlike patina, this will produce colors other than black. Mix in hot (not boiling) water according to manufacturer's directions in a disposable container; mix a weak solution for a light color with warm hues and a strong solution if deep black colors are desired.

Once desired color is achieved, rinse the pieces in cold water and to stop further oxidation, dip the clasps in a weak solution (1:4) of baking soda and water.

Don't be afraid to dip the clasps several times: the pieces can always later be lightened, and sometimes unsuspected colors, including purple, will appear after several dips.

**Hard-boiled egg:** If you are adverse to the toxicity of patina and liver of sulfur, you can jump-start the natural oxidation process of sterling silver using a hard-boiled egg:

Hard-boil an egg until cooked (about 10 to 15 minutes), place it in an airtight container while still warm, and smash it a few times.

Hang the clasp to be colored above the egg so that it does not have direct contact; to do so, string the clasp onto the thread, tape one end of the thread to each side of the container's rim, and place the lid on the container. Color typically develops within 24 to 36 hours. Repeat entire process if a deeper color is desired.

3~ **FINISHING.** Remove the sewing threads. If desired, use a polishing cloth to buff the pieces and to lighten the color. If you wish to remove a large amount of color, first polish with #0000 steel wool.

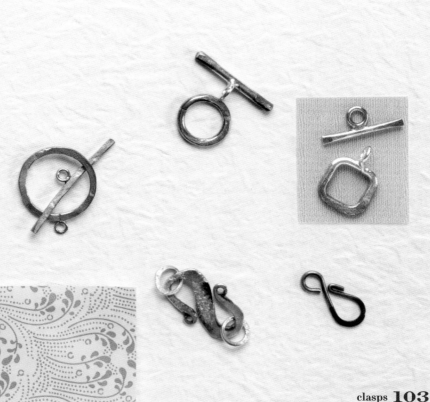

*midnight orbit*

*au naturel*

*antique hues*

*silver blues*

# orbital endings

Mimic the circular form of your necklace or bracelet with a closure made of flexible rings studded with beads. Make two rings and tie them together with fabric or make just one and attach your strand to it with a lobster clasp or hook.

## *au naturel*

**MATERIALS**

6 light green/brown 4mm fire-polished rounds

4 serpentine 7x5mm faceted rondelles

2 antique copper 2mm crimp tubes

1 amber/pink/green ½ x 9½" (1.3 x 24 cm) piece of cotton fabric with tapered ends

60" (152.5 cm) of copper satin .018 beading wire

1~ **RING.** Make 1 ring by looping the beading wire:

**Stringing:** Use the wire to string 1–3 beads and pass through the first bead again to form a 1" (2.5 cm) loop, leaving a 2" (5 cm) tail. Wrap the wire around the previous loop, string 1 bead, continue to weave through the previous loop, and pass through the second bead strung. Pull the wire snug. Repeat until all the beads have been added and 5 to 6 loops have been made, continuing to weave the wire through the previously formed loops and occasionally passing through previously strung beads.

2~ **FINISHING.** Work the wire around the loop so that it exits near the tail. String 1 crimp tube and use the tail wire to pass back through the tube. Snug the wires.

*Note: If you need more room to maneuver your tools, temporarily slide the beads aside during crimping.*

Repeat Steps 1 and 2 for a second ring. Use the fabric to tie the rings together after stringing your necklace or bracelet.

## silver blues

{see clasp on p. 104 and at far right}

**MATERIALS**

6 satin AB 4mm crystal bicones

4 amazonite 9mm faceted rounds

1 sterling silver 15mm round push clasp

4 sterling silver 1mm crimp tubes

72" (183 cm) of silver-plated .015 beading wire

1~ **RINGS.** Repeat Steps 1 and 2 of the Au Naturel clasp, stringing 2 crimp tubes instead of 1. For a suggestion on how to incorporate this clasp into a necklace or bracelet, see the sidebar at right.

## midnight orbit

{ see clasp on p. 104 and at far right}

**MATERIALS**

3 tourmaline 3mm crystal bicones

4 Montana blue 3mm crystal bicones

14 black AB 4mm faceted pressed-glass
  vintage nailhead coins

3 black AB 8mm faceted pressed-glass
  vintage nailhead coins

1 sterling silver 2mm crimp tube

1 sterling silver 7x16mm lobster clasp

30" (76 cm) of silver-plated .015 beading wire

1~ **RING.** Repeat Steps 1 and 2 of the Au Naturel clasp, making only 1 ring.

For a suggestion on how to incorporate this clasp into a necklace or bracelet, see the sidebar at right.

## antique hues

{see clasp on p. 104 and at lower right}

**MATERIALS**

11 dusty rose 3mm fire-polished rounds

3 dusty purple 6mm fire-polished rounds

16 antique bronze 4mm cogged heishi washers

1 antique bronze 18x21mm clasp hook

2 antique bronze 2mm crimp beads

36" (91.5 cm) of gold satin .015 beading wire

1~ **RING.** Repeat Steps 1 and 2 of the Au Naturel clasp, stringing 2 crimp tubes instead of 1. For a suggestion on how to incorporate this clasp into a necklace or bracelet, see the sidebar at right.

▼ *Use silver-plated .015 beading wire to string the* **silver blues** *clasp with additional amazonite 9mm faceted rounds and satin AB 4mm crystal bicones; suspend them on the wire by flattening sterling silver 1mm crimp tubes on each side of the beads.*

**stringing** *suggestions*

▼ *Use silver-plated .015 beading wire to string the* **midnight orbit** *clasp with onyx 13×18mm flat ovals, silver 6mm faceted pressed-glass vintage nailhead coins, and additional black AB 4mm nailhead beads.*

▼ *Use gold satin .015 beading wire to string the* **antique hues** *clasp with additional antique bronze 4mm cogged heishi washers and dusty rose 3mm and dusty purple 6mm fire-polished rounds.*

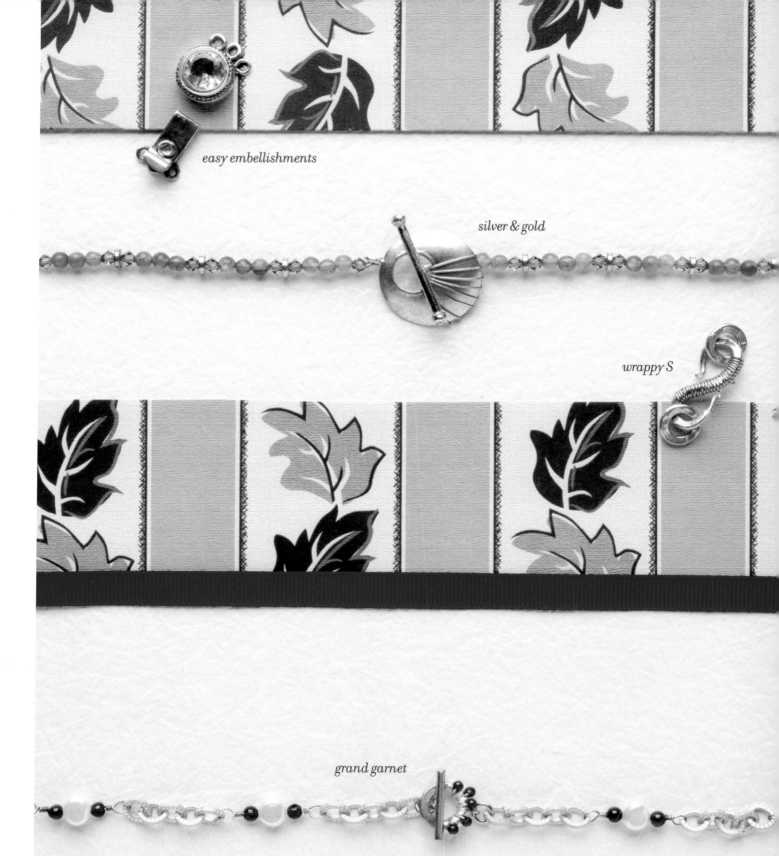

*easy embellishments*

*silver & gold*

*wrappy S*

*grand garnet*

# wrap it up

Smooth wire and shiny beads can dress up any simple clasp. With just a few wraps, you can make a customized closure to coordinate with your beaded creation. Why settle for something simple when you could have something sensational?

## *silver & gold*

**MATERIALS**

1 Thai silver 25x30mm round toggle clasp with off-center opening

Double-sided craft tape

12" (30.5 cm) of gold-filled 24-gauge wire

1~ **PREPARATION.** Place small pieces of double-sided craft tape on the back side of the ring half of the clasp in the place you wish to wrap the wire.

2~ **WRAPPING.** Fold the wire in half and pass one end through the clasp. Pull the wire ends so that the inside of the fold is tight against the inside of the clasp.

Holding the wire fold in place, wrap one end around one side of the ring, away from the center fold; as the wire passes the back, press the wire into the tape.

Repeat three times, spacing the wraps just under $1/8$" (3 mm) apart on the outside of the ring and just under $1/16$" (2 mm) apart on the inside of the ring.

End the last wrap on the back, fold the tail toward the center, trim to ¼" (6 mm), and tuck it under the previous wraps.

Repeat for the other side of the clasp, using the other half of the wire.

3~ **FINISHING.** For a suggestion on how to incorporate this clasp into a necklace or bracelet, see the sidebar on p. 111.

## grand garnet

{see clasp on p. 108 and at lower far right}

**MATERIALS**

5 garnet 3mm rounds

1 gold vermeil 13x16mm toggle clasp

Double-sided craft tape

12" (30.5 cm) of silver 26-gauge craft wire

**1~ PREPARATION.** Place small pieces of double-sided craft tape on the top of the ring half of the clasp, starting at the base of the clasp near the soldered ring and extending about ³/₈" (1 cm) to each side, or until about half of the ring is covered.

**2~ WRAPPING.** Wrap the wire around the clasp as for the Silver & Gold clasp, starting on one side of the clasp's soldered ring and keeping the wraps close together:

Wrap four to five times, string 1 garnet, slide it down to the clasp so that it rests on top of the clasp, and press into the tape. Wrapping four to five times again, string 1 garnet, press it into the tape, and make three more wraps. Tuck the wire tail under a previous wrap on the back and trim.

Repeat entire step for the other side of the clasp, using the other half of the wire, only begin by stringing 1 garnet and placing it as close to the soldered ring as possible.

**3~ FINISHING.** For a suggestion on how to incorporate this clasp into a necklace or bracelet, see the sidebar at far right.

### ❧ Tips

► *If you are worried about the wire tails coming loose, snagging, or unwrapping, simply coat the end of the tail with jeweler's cement.*

► *The craft tape is used to aid in the construction of the pieces but is not essential to it's function- ality, so don't worry if the tape loses tackiness over time.*

## wrappy S

**MATERIALS**

12 silver galvanized size 11° hex-cut seed beads

1 Thai silver 12x27mm hammered S-clasp

Double-sided craft tape

8" (20.5 cm) of copper 24-gauge wire

**1~ PREPARATION.** Place small pieces of double-sided craft tape on the top of the clasp, covering the center ¾" (2 cm). To make space for the wire and to ease wrapping, use the flat-nose pliers to open the clasp.

**2~ WRAPPING.** Fold and attach the wire to the center of the clasp as for the Silver & Gold clasp. Wrap once, string 2 seed beads, slide them down to the clasp so they rest on top of it, and press into the tape.

Make one wrap, string 2 seed beads, and press them into the tape; repeat once. Tightly wrap the wire around the clasp six to seven more times and trim the wire.

Repeat entire step for the other side of the clasp, using the other half of the wire and omitting the first wrap.

## easy embellishments

**MATERIALS**

35–45 purple size 15° charlottes

1 sterling silver 15x24mm round box clasp with stone inlay

Double-sided craft tape

9" (23 cm) of silver 26-gauge craft wire

G-S Hypo Cement

1~ **PREPARATION.** Trim a strip of craft tape to fit the height of the box clasp; wrap it around the outside edge of the clasp.

2~ **WRAPPING.** Press one end of the wire to the tape, at the base of the clasp and make one full wrap. String enough charlottes to fit around the base, slide them down, and press into the tape.

Continue wrapping the wire around the base three to four more times, until you reach the top edge of the tape. Trim the wire and press the wire end into the tape. If desired, place a small amount of cement on the wire tails.

▲ *Pair the* **silver & gold** *clasp with labradorite 4mm rounds, smoked topaz 4mm crystal bicones, and silver 5×1mm spacers.*

## stringing *suggestions*

▼ *Pair the* **grand garnet** *clasp with gold-filled 6×8mm textured oval chain; break the sections of chain with wrapped-loop links made with sterling silver 24-gauge wire, cream 8mm pearls, and garnet 4mm rounds.*

*springtime
simplicity*

*yellow seeds
& sprouts*

*budding
bellflowers*

*ruby flowers*

# millefiori mesh

At the heart of these organic clasps are cleverly embellished mesh screens. Use needle and thread to adorn the screens with a spattering of seed, flower, and drop beads before mounting them onto box clasps.

**TOOLBOX**

Scissors

Size 10 or 12 beading needle

Fine-point permanent marker

Round-nose pliers

Chain-nose pliers

## *springtime simplicity*

### MATERIALS

2 g mix of matte and luster size 15° and 11° seed beads in light and dark teal, green, and teal-lined clear

1 imitation rhodium 18mm 3-strand box clasp with blank mesh screen insert

Pale blue nylon beading thread

1~ **PREPARATION.** Use the chain-nose pliers to gently open the tabs along the top edge of the clasp and use the marker to mark the placement of the tabs. Avoid stitching over these marks so that the tabs can sit flush to the screen when the embellished screen is reinserted.

2~ **STITCHING.** To begin stitching, pass the needle, threaded with 4' (1.2 m) of thread, through a hole in the center of the screen, take the needle down through an adjacent hole. Knot twice, leaving a short tail. Use the following guidelines when stitching:

**Seed stitch:** Bring the needle up near the center of the screen, string 1 seed bead, and pass down through an adjacent hole

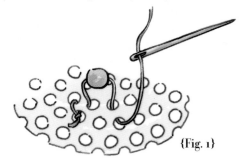

{Fig. 1}

Bring the needle back up through a different adjacent hole {Fig. 1} and repeat stitching, choosing bead colors at random.

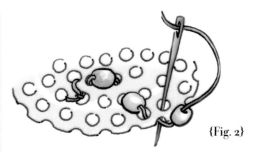

{Fig. 2}

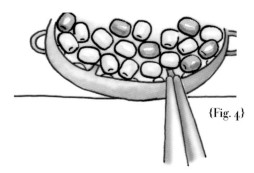

{Fig. 4}

**&Tips**

➤ *The box clasps used here are 3-strand. However, if your necklace or bracelet calls for only 1 or 2 strands, simply trim off the extra loops of the clasp using wire cutters or tin snips. Smooth the cut edges with sandpaper.*

➤ *If you find it hard to keep tension on the thread after stringing a flower or other large bead, take a few stitches without any beads into adjacent holes of the screen to keep the thread tight.*

**Working on the edge:** Since some of the holes along the edge of the screen are not whole, make sure you always stitch from the center of the screen outward (stitching to the side may cause the thread to slip over the edge). When making the next stitch, bring the needle up toward the center again {Fig. 2}.

**Fixing sideways beads:** If you find that the hole on the side of a seed bead (instead of the top) is showing, you can turn the bead the right direction by bringing the needle to the front and passing through several adjacent seed beads (including the sideways bead) before taking the needle to the back {Fig. 3}.

{Fig. 3}

**3~ MOUNTING.** Press the screen insert back in place, aligning the marked holes with the tabs. Place the clasp near the edge of your worktable.

With the round-nose pliers closed and pointing up and your hand off the side of the table, press the tabs toward the center of the clasp to fold the tabs back down and secure the insert {Fig. 4}.

**4~ FINISHING.** For a suggestion on how to incorporate this clasp into a necklace or bracelet, see the sidebar at far right.

## *ruby flowers*

{see project on p. 112 and at lower far right}

### MATERIALS

1 g of cranberry AB size 11° seed beads

10–12 matte ruby AB 5x2mm pressed-glass flowers

3–5 crystal celsian 6x4mm pressed-glass baby bellflowers

1 antique copper 18mm 3-strand box clasp with blank mesh screen insert

Red nylon beading thread

**1~ CLASP.** Repeat Steps 1–3 for the Springtime Simplicity clasp; however, when working with the flowers, take the first stitch by stringing 1 ruby flower and 1 seed bead. Pass back through the flower before taking the needle to the back.

Evenly space 9–11 more ruby flowers and 3–5 crystal celsian flowers around the screen and fill the area between the flowers with seed beads as before.

**2~ FINISHING.** For a suggestion on how to incorporate this clasp into a necklace or bracelet, see the sidebar at far right.

## budding bellflowers

### MATERIALS

1 g of purple-lined clear size 11° seed beads

22–26 prairie green 6mm glass lentil beads

12 green luster 6x4mm pressed-glass baby bellflowers

1 antique brass 22mm 3-strand box clasp with blank mesh screen insert

Pale blue nylon beading thread

Repeat Steps 1–3 for the Springtime Simplicity clasp, anchoring flowers with seed beads according to the Ruby Flowers clasp instructions.

Embellish the screen with the green flowers and the areas between the flowers with the lentil beads. Fill small areas between the flowers and lentils with seed beads.

## yellow seeds & sprouts

### MATERIALS

25–30 yellow matte 4x6mm glass teardrops

18–22 yellow/pale blue 4x6mm glass teardrops

8–12 yellow matte 3x8mm pressed-glass daggers

1 silver-plated 22mm 3-strand box clasp with blank mesh screen insert

Yellow nylon beading thread

Repeat Steps 1–3 for the Springtime Simplicity clasp, adding teardrops and daggers at random.

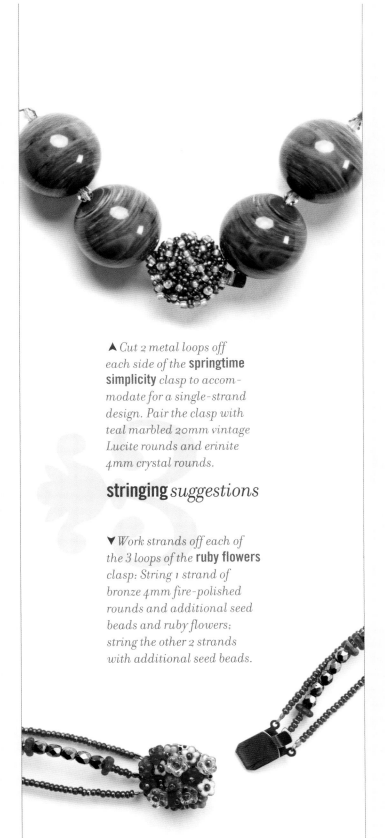

▲ *Cut 2 metal loops off each side of the* **springtime simplicity** *clasp to accommodate for a single-strand design. Pair the clasp with teal marbled 20mm vintage Lucite rounds and erinite 4mm crystal rounds.*

## stringing *suggestions*

▼ *Work strands off each of the 3 loops of the* **ruby flowers** *clasp: String 1 strand of bronze 4mm fire-polished rounds and additional seed beads and ruby flowers; string the other 2 strands with additional seed beads.*

# FINISHED PROJECTS ⚜

In the following pages you'll find six fun, fresh designs that combine your new component-making skills with basic wireworking and stringing techniques. From a bracelet with dozens of personalized charms to a lush multistrand necklace with a bead-embroidered cabochon or a funky necklace dripping with vintage Lucite, you'll see how easy and fun it is to combine custom-made components with your favorite beads and findings.

For more
handmade
custom
clasps like the
one shown
here, see
p.112.

# forest floor necklace

Rich moss-colored beads with patches of small flower dangles will remind you of walking in a deep forest. Strands made of simple links and decorative dangles send you running for your wireworking tools.

1~ **CLASP.** Repeat Steps 1–3 for the Springtime Simplicity clasp and stitch flowers according to the Ruby Flowers clasp instructions (see pp. 113–114); embellish the mesh with 7 evenly spaced flowers and medium or dark purple seed beads. Fill the area between the flowers with green seed beads. Cut 2 metal loops off each side of the clasp to accommodate for this single-strand necklace; smooth the cut edges with the sandpaper.

2~ **STRANDS.** Cut the wire into two 2" (5 cm) pieces and sixteen 1½" (3.8 cm) pieces. Use 2" (5 cm) of wire to form a wrapped loop that attaches to one half of the clasp; string 1 moss green matte 11mm round and form a simple loop. *Use 1½" (3.8 cm) of wire to form a simple loop that attaches to the free end of the previous link; string 1 moss green 17mm round and form a simple loop. Use 1½" (3.8 cm) of wire to form a simple loop that attaches to the free end of the previous link; string 1 moss green matte 11mm round and form a simple loop. Repeat from * three times. Attach the chain to the free end of the last link.

Repeat entire step, attaching the first link to the other half of the clasp and the last link to the free end of the chain.

3~ **DANGLES.** Make all of the dangles before attaching them to the chain:

**Fancy flowers:** Use a ball-end head pin to string 1 flower and 1 medium or dark purple seed bead; form a simple loop. Repeat thirteen times for a total of 14 dangles.

**Plain flowers:** Use a natural brass head pin to string 1 medium or dark seed bead and 1 flower; form a simple loop. Repeat five times for a total of 6 dangles.

**Rounds:** Use a ball-end head pin to string 1 moss green 17mm round and form a simple loop. Repeat with the remaining ball-end head pins and rounds for a total of 12 dangles.

**Finishing:** Attach the moss green 17mm round dangle to the center link of the chain. Attach all of the remaining dangles to the chain, positioning them as desired and adding the largest beads near the center link; attach flower dangles to each chain link so that they are scattered throughout.

See additional tools needed on p. 113

**TOOLBOX**

Wire cutters

Round-nose pliers

Chain-nose pliers

See additional tools needed on p. 113

**MATERIALS**

2 g total of size 11° seed beads in medium purple, dark purple, and green

27 pale green marbled 8x3mm pressed-glass flowers

4 matte moss green marbled 7mm vintage Lucite rounds

3 moss green marbled 9mm vintage Lucite rounds

12 matte moss green marbled 11mm vintage Lucite rounds

2 pale mint green marbled 11mm vintage Lucite rounds

9 moss green marbled 17mm vintage Lucite rounds

1 antique brass 17mm 3-strand box clasp with blank mesh metal insert

6 natural brass 1½" (38mm) head pins

26 brass 2½" (65mm) head pins with 3mm ball ends

1½" ([3.8 cm], 5 links) of natural brass 10mm round chain

Pale purple nylon beading thread

28" (71 cm) of gunmetal 20-gauge craft wire

Super fine 400-grit sandpaper

**FINISHED SIZE**

19¼" (49 cm)

*For more handmade custom clasps like the one shown here, see p. 98.*

# eye candy bracelet

Let beads crafted of Lucite and lampworked glass be the stars of the show. Any way you wear it, you're sure to have your entire wrist encircled with color thanks to a hand-made beaded hook-and-eye clasp.

**TOOLBOX**

Wire cutters

Crimping pliers

See additional tools needed on p. 99

**MATERIALS**

18 turquoise size 15° charlottes

4 red/blue spotted 10x7mm lampworked glass rondelles

2 red/blue bumpy 13x10mm lampworked glass rondelles

1 dusty rose 11mm vintage Lucite round

6 aqua/white striped 10x17mm vintage Lucite ovals

2 sterling silver 2mm crimp tubes

2 sterling silver 3mm crimp covers

9½" (24 cm) of sterling silver 20-gauge dead-soft wire

9½" (24 cm) of .019 beading wire

**FINISHED SIZE**

8¼" (21 cm)

1~ **CLASP.** Make a hook-and-eye clasp that incorporates beads:

**Hook with wrapped loop:** Follow directions for the Filigree Fun hook (p. 101), stringing 1 spotted rondelle (in place of the 6mm round).

**Eye with wrapped-loop link:** Follow directions for the Filigree Fun eye, stringing 1 spotted rondelle (in place of the crystal and filigree rounds).

**Hammering:** Finish as for the Sweet Spots clasp (p. 100).

2~ **STRINGING.** Use the beading wire to string 1 crimp tube, 9 charlottes, and one half of the clasp; pass back through the tube. Snug the beads so that the charlottes cover the wire that passes through the clasp. Crimp the crimp tube and cover the tube with a crimp cover. String 1 oval, 1 bumpy rondelle, 1 oval, 1 spotted rondelle, 1 oval, 1 dusty rose round, 1 oval, 1 spotted rondelle, 1 oval, 1 bumpy rondelle, 1 oval, 1 crimp tube, 9 charlottes, and the other half of the clasp; pass back through the crimp tube. Snug the beads so that the charlottes cover the wire that passes through the clasp. Crimp the crimp tube and cover the tube with a crimp cover.

For more
handmade
custom
pendants like
the one shown
here, see
p. 46.

## ❧Tips

➤ If the beads are in a
hank, you can quickly
transfer the beads to the
thread without using
a needle: Tie the hank
thread and FireLine
together using a tight
square knot and slide the
beads over the knot, onto
the FireLine.

➤ If the bead cap does
not fit snugly around
the top of the seed bead
strands, use the chain-
nose pliers to gently bend
the bottom of the bead
cap closed.

# santa fe necklace

Matching cabochons give this necklace a perfect sense of balance. In colors reminiscent of Southwestern art, the multiple strands of seed beads are gathered into sweet bead caps and feel oh-so-good on your neck.

**1~ PENDANT.** Repeat Steps 1 and 2 for the Vintage Vogue pendant (see p. 47) using the beading foundation and turquoise beading thread. When working Pass 1, add kelly green seed beads and leave enough room between the beads to accommodate for the teardrops (18 evenly spaced teardrops were used to surround the cabochon shown here). Add the teardrops in Pass 2.

**Bail:** Position the bail so that it overhangs the top of the pendant by ¼" (6 mm). Use the turquoise beading thread to stitch into the foundation and around the bail several times to secure it flat against the felt.

**Adhere:** Repeat as in Step 3 of the Vintage Vogue pendant.

**Backing:** Cut an oval out of the teal felt to the size of the back of the pendant. Make a small slit in the back to accommodate for the loop of the bail. Cement in place, covering the half of the bail that is stitched down. Close the bail and use the jump ring to join the loops of the bail.

**2~ STRINGING.** Add strands to the pendant:
**Seed bead only strands:** With the FireLine still attached to the spool, thread the needle and string 16½" (42 cm) of turquoise seed beads and the bail. Slide the bail to the center of the strand; trim the thread, leaving a 3" (7.5 cm) tail at each end and using the bead stops to hold the beads in place. Repeat twice using turquoise seed beads and twice using turquoise charlottes for a total of 5 strands; make each strand ⅛–¼" (3–6 mm) longer or shorter than the first for a layered look.

**Teardrop strands:** Repeat as before using turquoise seed beads and adding the remaining drops at random near the center of the strands. Repeat four times for a total of 5 strands, using up all of the teardrops.

**Finishing:** Use 2" (5 cm) of wire to form a wrapped loop. Remove 1 bead stop; working with 2 threads at a time, use square knots to tie all 10 thread tails to the wrapped loop; trim and cement the knots. Use the wire to string the wide end of 1 bead cap (to cover the knots) and 1 turquoise seed bead; form a wrapped loop that attaches to one half of the clasp.

Remove the second bead stop and repeat finishing instructions, being sure to snug the beads when tying the threads to the wrapped loop.

## TOOLBOX
Scissors

Size 12 beading needle

Wire cutters

Chain-nose pliers

Round-nose pliers

2 bead stops

See additional tools needed on p. 47

## MATERIALS
33" (84 cm) of turquoise size 15° charlottes

11' (3.5 m) (or 1 hank) of turquoise size 11° seed beads

18 kelly green size 11° seed beads

21 turquoise 4x6mm glass teardrops

32 turquoise mottled 5x9mm glass teardrops

1 coral 18x25mm floral pressed-glass cabochon

2 Thai silver 12x10mm flower bead caps

1 sterling silver 4x26mm donut bail

1 sterling silver/coral 18x38mm box clasp with floral pressed-glass inlay

1 sterling silver 4mm jump ring

Smoke FireLine 6 lb beading thread

Turquoise nylon beading thread

4" (10 cm) of sterling silver 24-gauge wire

2 x 2" (5 x 5 cm) piece of Lacy's Stiff Stuff beading foundation

2 x 2" (5 x 5 cm) piece of teal felt

G-S Hypo Cement

## FINISHED SIZE
18¾" (47.5 cm)

*For more handmade custom pendants like the one shown here, see p. 33.*

# floral romance necklace

Dimensional chain (comprised of an overabundant amount of chain loops) adds lacy flair and delicacy to the pineapple quartz links. The lace image of the pendant is the perfect feminine touch.

1~ **PENDANT.** Follow the directions and see the additional tools and materials needed on p. 33 to make a white 32mm polymer clay coin pendant with an image of black lace; use 1" (2.5 cm) of wire to form a wrapped-loop hanger and cement the tail into the top of the pendant.

2~ **STRANDS.** Cut the remaining wire into nine 2" (5 cm) pieces. Cut the chain into two 10-link sections and six 12-link sections; save 6 of the 5mm closed rings that fall from the chain.

**Chain links:** Use a silver jump ring to attach one 10-link section of chain to one half of the clasp. *Use 2" (5 cm) of wire to form a wrapped loop that attaches to the free end of the previous chain; string 1 pineapple quartz and form a wrapped loop that attaches to one 12-link section of chain. Repeat from * twice. Use 2" (5 cm) of wire to form a wrapped loop that attaches to the free end of the previous chain; string 1 pineapple quartz and form a wrapped loop. Set aside this half of the strand.

Repeat to form the second half of the strand, attaching the jump ring to the other half of the clasp.

**Focal:** Use 2" (5 cm) of wire to form a wrapped loop that attaches to the free ends of the pineapple quartz links at the end of the 2 strands; string 1 pineapple quartz and form a wrapped loop that attaches to the pendant (this creates a Y-shaped necklace).

3~ **DANGLES AND CHARMS.** Decorate the pendant with dangles and charms, attaching them to the pineapple-quartz links that form the Y-shaped center of the necklace above the pendant:

**Pineapple quartz:** Use a head pin to string 1 pineapple quartz and form a simple loop that attaches to one of the pineapple-quartz links. Repeat twice for a total of 3 pineapple-quartz dangles.

**Rings:** Use 1 round gunmetal jump ring to attach 2 metal 5mm closed rings to one of the pineapple-quartz links. Repeat twice to attach the 4 remaining closed rings.

**Charms:** Use 1 oval gunmetal jump ring to attach 1 charm to one loop of the pineapple-quartz link. Repeat to attach the remaining charm to the other loop of the link.

**TOOLBOX**

Wire cutters
Chain-nose pliers
Round-nose pliers

**MATERIALS**

12 pineapple quartz 6mm faceted rounds
2 metal 4x9mm cone charms
Glittery white Fimo polymer modeling clay
1 sterling silver 12x26mm floral oval box clasp
3 sterling silver 1" (25mm) head pins
6 metal 5mm closed rings (cut free from the chain)
2 gunmetal 3x4mm oval jump rings
3 gunmetal 5mm jump rings
2 sterling silver 5mm jump rings
12" (30.5 cm) of silver 5mm chain with decorative loops
19" (48.5 cm) of sterling silver 24-gauge wire

**FINISHED SIZE**

19¼" (49 cm)

For more handmade custom collage charms like the ones shown here, see p.76.

# a love of travel charm bracelet

Recall meaningful journeys or dream of places you want to visit and make charms reminiscent of these adventures. String them with similarly themed premade charms and carry your story on your wrist.

**1~ COLLAGE CHARMS.** See p. 77 for additional charm-making materials and follow the instructions to make 6 charms using the materials below:

**Map Italia:** Embellish an antique copper 18x30mm teardrop bezel with a map of Italy and a ring of 60–62 gold size 15° charlottes; seal with epoxy. Attach 1 antique copper 7mm jump ring to the top.

**Hawaiian Islands charm:** Embellish an antique brass 18x30mm teardrop bezel with a map of the Hawaiian islands and a ring of 40–44 pearly blue size 11° seed beads; seal with epoxy. Attach 1 antique brass 9mm jump ring to the top.

**Watch parts charm:** Embellish imitation rhodium and antique brass 30mm round bezels with scrapbooking paper and antique watch parts; seal with Diamond Glaze. Attach 1 antique copper 6mm jump ring to the imitation rhodium bezel and 1 antique brass 9mm jump ring to the brass bezel.

**Love charm:** Embellish 1 pewter 15x22mm teardrop bezel with scrapbooking paper, paper with the word "love" printed, stickers, and gold, teal, and red size 15° charlottes; seal with epoxy.

**Diamond and oval charm:** Embellish silver 14x18mm diamond and Thai silver 8x18mm pointed-oval charms with scrapbooking paper (a portion of a compass was used for the pointed-oval charm); seal with Diamond Glaze.

**2~ DANGLE AND OTHER CHARMS.**

**Dangle:** Use the head pin to string the pinecone bead and form a wrapped loop.

**Other charms:** If the premade charms hang the wrong direction when strung, attach 1 or 3 jump rings. You may also wish to attach jump rings to other charms that you want to hang farther away from the strung beads of the bracelet.

**3~ STRINGING.** Attach the beading wire to one half of the clasp using a crimp tube. String 3 seed beads. String beads in the following order, stringing charms between the beads as desired: {1 yellow glass round, 1 teal Lucite round, 1 striped round, and 1 teal Lucite round} six times. String 1 yellow round, 3 seed beads, 1 crimp tube, and the other half of the clasp; pass back through the tube and crimp.

TOOLBOX
Scissors
Size 10 or 12 beading needle
Wire cutters
Crimping pliers
Round-nose pliers
Flat-nose pliers
See additional tools needed on p. 77

MATERIALS
6 teal matte size 11° seed beads

7 matte yellow 5mm glass rounds

6 blue/yellow striped 8mm glass rounds

12 matte teal marbled 6mm vintage Lucite rounds

About 18 assorted sterling silver, pewter, and antique brass and copper 10–25mm charms and beads including hearts, animals, buildings, and people

7 pewter, imitation rhodium, and antique copper and brass 17–30mm teardrop, round, pointed-oval, and diamond sealed collage charms (see Step 1 and p. 77 for materials)

1 antique brass 12x21mm lock-and-key toggle clasp

1 copper 1½" (38mm) head pin

20–25 assorted sterling silver, gunmetal, and antique brass and copper 5–9mm jump rings

2 gold-filled 2mm crimp tubes

10" (25.5 cm) of copper satin .018 beading wire

FINISHED SIZE
8" (20.5 cm)

*For more handmade custom collages like the one shown here, see p. 76.*

# love bees necklace

Show your eclectic side with your newfound collage skills. Make a link with a pair of bees and resin powder, add a heart charm, and string with beautiful and simple vintage Lucite and nailhead beads.

**1~ PENDANT.** See p. 77 and follow the instructions to make a collage in the link's bezel, partially filling the bezel with polymer clay, adhering a circle of pink paper to the clay, and placing the bee charms (trim the loop off the charms, if needed) on top of the paper. Seal using Amazing Glaze (See pp. 79–81). Use the oval jump ring to attach the heart charm to the bottom of the link. Attach all of the 4mm jump rings to the top of the link.

**2~ CLASP.** If desired, darken the 18mm ring using black patina (see p. 103).

**3~ STRINGING.** Use the beading wire to string 1 crimp tube, 13 charlottes, and the 18mm ring. Pass back through the crimp tube. Snug the beads so that the charlottes cover the wire. Crimp the tube and cover the crimp tube with a crimp cover. String {1 fire-polished round, 1 nailhead, 1 Lucite round, and 1 nailhead} six times. String {3 charlottes, 1 nailhead, 1 Lucite round, and 1 nailhead} three times.

String 5 charlottes and the 4mm jump rings of the pendant. Snug the beads so that the charlottes cover the wire that passes through the jump rings.

Repeat entire step for the other half of the necklace, reversing the stringing sequence and attaching the clasp hook at the end of the wire.

## TOOLBOX

Crimping pliers

Wire cutters

Chain-nose pliers

Scissors

See additional tools needed on p. 77

## MATERIALS

49 gold size 15° charlottes

12 clear/gold mirror 4mm fire-polished rounds

36 silver 6mm faceted pressed-glass vintage nailhead coins

18 matte cranberry 9mm vintage Lucite rounds

1 sterling silver 18mm textured ring

1 sterling silver 21x30mm square link with circle bezel

2 brass 7x5mm bee charms

1 brass 15mm heart charm

1 sterling silver 13x21mm clasp hook

1 antique brass 3x4mm oval jump ring

3 antique brass 4mm jump rings

2 gold-filled 2mm crimp tubes

2 gold-filled 3mm crimp tube covers

21" (53.5 cm) of .019 beading wire

Pink scrapbooking paper for bezel background

Amazing Glaze resin powder

Acid-free white craft glue

Parchment paper

Polymer clay

Liver of sulfur (optional)

## FINISHED SIZE

18½" (47 cm)

# beading & wireworking 101

## bead types

**CRYSTAL BEADS** are made of faceted leaded glass. Use beading wire or braided beading thread when stringing crystals as the sharp edges of the holes in the beads may cut through nylon beading thread.

### PEARLS

**Freshwater pearls** are real pearls cultivated by inserting irritants into farmed oysters; nacre coating is formed around these irritants, resulting in unevenly sized pearls.

**Crystal pearls** are imitation pearls with a crystal core and thus have a regular, consistent shape.

### GLASS

**Pressed-glass** is a general term for beads that have been formed while the glass is in a molten state; the shape is most often achieved by stamping the hot glass or pressing it through a mold.

**Fire-polished** beads are made of faceted Czech pressed-glass and are an affordable alternative to crystals.

---

**Lampworked** beads begin as narrow rods of cold glass. The glass is heated and spun onto a mandrel over a flame.

**Nailheads** are vintage pressed-glass coins. Their flat bottom and faceted surface give them the appearance of a nailhead that has been hammered several times.

**Cabochons** have at least one flat side and since they do not have holes, they are most commonly glued to a foundation material or encrusted in seed beads using beadweaving stitches.

### CLAY

**Polymer** beads are made from modeling clay that has been baked at a lower temperature than ceramic beads; they commonly have a matte finish.

**Ceramic** beads are clay beads that have been fired at a high temperature and often coated with a decorative glaze and/or handpainted designs.

**Precious metal clay (PMC)** findings and beads, also referred to as fine silver, are formed from a claylike material that becomes 99.9 percent fine silver when fired.

## NATURAL

**Wood** beads are some of the most affordable beads, made out of a variety of woods and treated with an array of finishes.

**Horn and bone** beads are handmade beads that usually come from Indonesia and the Philippines.

**Stone** beads are found in a countless number of varieties but most large sizes are heavy, so be sure to use a strong beading wire. Stones used in this book include labradorite, amazonite, citrine, serpentine, garnet, aquamarine, honey opal, and lemon, pineapple, rutilated, and smoky quartz.

**Coral** beads are made of real coral that has been polished smooth or left in its natural branch form.

## PLASTIC

**Vintage Lucite** beads, also referred to as acrylic, are strong, durable beads made out of a trademarked thermoplastic resin. Jewelry made of this material was most popular in the early 1950s, and although the material is still being produced today, most of the beads on the market are from factories that closed in the 1970s, making the pieces truly vintage.

## SEED BEADS

**Seed beads** are often sold prestrung in bundles called *hanks*. A typical hank of size 11° seed beads measures about 10" (25.5 cm) long (20" [51 cm] of beads per loop) and hanks of size 15° charlottes are about 6" (15 cm) long (12" [30.5 cm] of beads per loop); one hank commonly consists of 12 loops of beads. The beads are temporarily strung on thin thread and must be restrung or transferred onto a stronger thread or wire.

*Aught* describes a seed bead's size and is represented by a small degree symbol. The exact origin of this symbol is unknown, but it is thought to have once referred to how many beads occupy an inch when strung side by side. Although this does not correlate to the length of today's inch, the size distinctions are still widely used. They are sized on an inverse scale: the larger the number, the smaller the bead.

**Czech seed** beads are shaped like donuts and are slightly irregular. They are found in a wide variety of sizes, from a large 7° to a very tiny 20°.

**Cylinder** beads (not pictured) (Delica, Toho, and Magnifica brands) are perfectly cylindrical, consistently shaped beads with thin walls and large holes.

**Japanese seed** beads (not pictured) share characteristics of Czech and cylinder beads, but are slightly more round due to a thicker wall.

**Charlottes** (shown on strand above) are seed beads that have been cut on one side and most commonly used in size 15°. This cut edge catches the light, creating a sparkly look.

**Triangle** beads have three distinct sides.

**Cube** beads have four sides and usually considerably large holes.

**Hex-cut** beads have six surfaces that reflect light, resulting in a shiny bead.

## MISCELLANEOUS

**Charms,** often found in metal and porcelain, are decorative elements that are commonly stamped with designs. They are hung by a loop on one end.

**Bezel settings** are metal charms with a deep rim, or bezel, around the edges. The rims are ideal for containing collage items that are to be covered with epoxy or resin (see p. 76).

**Links,** or connectors, are simply charms with two or more loops, used for connecting multiple strands, threads, or chains.

**Spacers** are used as decorative elements strung between larger beads.

**Cones** are cylindrical findings that taper to a point at one end. They are often used to neatly gather the ends of multiple strands: Use at least 2" (5 cm) of gauged wire to form a wrapped loop that attaches to the strands. Use the wire to string the wide end of the cone and form a second wrapped loop that attaches to a clasp.

# bead shapes

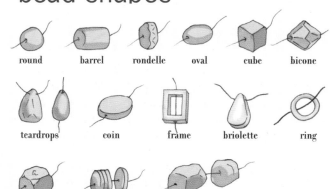

round    barrel    rondelle    oval    cube    bicone

teardrops    coin    frame    briolette    ring

cornerles cube    heishi    nuggets

# findings

## PINS

**Flat-end head** pins are the most common style of head pin. When a bead is strung on one, the flat end sits flush against the hole in the bead. If the gauge is not indicated, it is probably 24-gauge; this gauge is strong yet thin enough to accommodate most beads.

**Ball-end head** pins have round decorative tips.

**Eye pins** have a simple loop at one end so that they may be connected to other design elements.

## WIRE

**Gauge** indicates the size of the wire. Follow this simple rule: the lower the gauge number, the thicker the wire.

| | |
|---|---|
| 10 | ● |
| 12 | ● |
| 14 | ● |
| 16 | ● |
| 18 | ● |
| 20 | ● |
| 22 | ● |
| 24 | ● |
| 26 | ● |
| 28 | ● |

**Hard, half-hard,** and **dead-soft** refer to the "temper" (hardness or softness) of the wire. Half-hard is most commonly used for wrapped-loop links and dangles in stringing projects and should be used unless an alternate hardness is indicated. Wire is naturally "work-hardened" through manipulation. If over-worked, the wire will become brittle and break.

**Craft wire** is copper wire that has been permanently coated with a colored finish. This wire tends to be softer, so use light pressure when making simple and wrapped loops.

## RINGS & BAILS

**Jump rings** are small circles, squares, or rectangles of wire used as connectors. These rings can be opened and closed to string components.

**Closed rings** (also called soldered rings) serve the same purpose as jump rings but are soldered closed.

**Split rings** are similar to key rings: two overlapping loops of wire prevent the ring from being pulled open.

**Bail** is a general term for the hanger at the top of a pendant or a finding with a tubelike opening. Bails can be handmade out of wire (see p. 136) or sold as metal findings that consist of a large loop (that connects to the design's strand) and a small loop (that attaches to the end of a beading wire or other finding). Some bails have the appearance of claws (like the one shown here) and when closed, the prongs of the claws pass through a bead's hole.

**CHAIN** is available in a multitude of finishes, sizes, and shapes, including oval, round, and diamond. Most often the links are soldered and must be cut open. However, if the links are already split, they can be opened and closed like jump rings and no links are wasted.

## CLASPS

**Toggle** clasps have a bar on one side and a ring on the other. When making your own, follow this rule: The bar half of the clasp should be twice as long as the ring's opening is wide (otherwise the bar may slip through the ring). Since the bar must pass through the ring when attaching the necklace or bracelet, be sure to string at least ½" (1.3 cm) (or a little more than half the length of the bar) of small beads at the end of the strand before the bar.

**S-hook** clasps are made of an S-shaped wire permanently attached to a jump ring on one side; the S closes through a second jump ring on the opposite side.

**Box** clasps are shaped like a rectangle, square, or circular box on one end and have a bent metal tab on the other end that snaps into the box under its own tension. The tops often have stone, glass, pearl, or other decorative inlays.

**Lobster** clasps open and close like a claw and are great for connecting jewelry to chain.

**Hook-and-eye** clasps have a J-shaped hook on one side that connects to a loop (or ring) on the opposite side.

## CRIMPS AND CAPS

**Crimp tubes** and crimp beads secure beading wire to findings.

**Crimp covers** are hollow, partially opened beads that wrap around crimp tubes and beads to conceal them.

**Bead caps** are decorative cup-shaped elements strung snug up to the side of a bead.

## METAL FINISHES

**Filigree** components are delicate openwork designs, available in numerous metals and finishes.

**Gold-filled** beads and findings are made of base metal (an inexpensive, non-precious metal); the surface is then coated with $\frac{1}{10}$ of 12k gold.

**Vermeil** findings and beads are made of sterling silver that has been electroplated with gold.

**Thai silver** beads are handmade in Thailand by the Karen hill tribe. Thai silver is 99.5–99.9 percent silver.

**Sterling silver** beads and findings are 92.5 percent pure silver and 7.5 percent copper.

**Fine silver** beads see p. 131.

**Copper** beads and findings are 100 percent copper and thus may turn green as natural oxidation occurs over time. Because copper wire is inexpensive, it's great for practicing your wireworking skills. Findings labeled as antique copper have been slightly oxidized for an antique-looking finish.

**Brass** is an alloy that is typically 67 percent copper and 33 percent zinc. Findings sold as natural brass (right) have a deep brown finish whereas antique brass (left) components are lighter and more yellow in color.

**Gunmetal** is a general term for beads and findings with a black or dark gray color, which are made from an alloy of metals.

**Imitation rhodium** (not pictured) beads and findings have been electroplated to give the appearance of rhodium, a white-colored metallic element (symbol Rh), or silver.

# stringing materials

**Nylon beading threads,** (not pictured) such as C-Lon, Nymo, and Silamide, are most commonly used for lightweight beading projects.

**Braided beading thread,** (not pictured) such as FireLine is flexible like thread yet stronger and more resistant to breakage. Thus, it is a great choice when stringing sharp-holed beads like crystals. It is easiest to cut using children's Fiskars scissors.

**Nylon cord** (not pictured) has the look of natural waxed linen cord but is synthetic so the ends can be melted with a match, thread burner, or lighter to prevent fraying.

**Thread Heaven** thread conditioner is used with nylon beading thread to protect the thread from fraying and breakage and prevent tangling.

**Beading wire** (not pictured) is strong and flexible, most commonly secured with crimp tubes and beads, and is made of multiple thin steel wires that have been coated with nylon; the more strands of core wires used, the more flexible the beading wire becomes. The most common sizes are .019 and .018 (which are best used with 2mm crimp tubes) and .014 (which is best used with 1mm or 1x2mm crimp tubes and micro crimping pliers); see box on p. 137 for more information.

**Bead stops** are springlike findings that temporarily snap on to the end of beading wire to prevent spills while stringing.

**Beading needles** (not pictured) are used to string beads onto beading thread. They are long and thin to accommodate for the small holes of beads and because of this often bend easily. The most commonly used sizes are 10–13.

**A design board** (not pictured) is a valuable tool that prevents beads from rolling around your work surface, and the semicircle grooves allow you to visualize a design before it is strung.

# tools

## Wire or flush cutters
are used to cut both gauged wire and beading wire. Their sharp edges ensure that no burrs are left on the trimmed ends of the wire. Do not attempt to cut memory wire with your wire cutters because it will mar the edges of the cutter.

**Chain- and flat-nose pliers** are essential for opening and closing jump rings and manipulating wire. The inside jaws of both are flat and smooth. However, the outside edges of chain-nose pliers are round on the top and bottom and flat-nose pliers (shown here) are flat on both edges. Chain-nose pliers taper toward the tip, making them great for working with small links of chain and in other small spaces.

**Round-nose pliers** are used to make loops and curls in wire. Their conical jaws taper toward the tip so if a large loop is desired, position wire near the base of the jaw; for small loops, work the wire at the tips.

**Crimping pliers** are flat pliers that have two notches used to secure crimp tubes on beading wire: one notch is used to flatten crimp tubes and the other is used to fold the tube in half. They are available in three sizes: generally Micro pliers are used when working with 1mm wide tubes, regular for 2mm wide tubes, and Mighty for 3mm tubes.

**Hammers** (not pictured) are used to flatten and add texture to wire. Chasing hammers have one small end, called ball-peen, that is used to add texture and one large, flat end for flattening wire. Do not worry if you do not have a chasing hammer, any hammer from a hardware store with a small, smooth tip can be used to manipulate wire.

**Bench blocks** (not pictured) are flat, thick blocks of polished steel that protect your work surface when hammering. Their smooth surface also prevents wire from marring.

**Heat tools** (not pictured) are available at craft stores and are used by scrapbookers for melting embossing powder onto paper. They can heat to 650°F and should be used with caution.

# how to

## JUMP RINGS
Using two pairs of flat- or chain-nose pliers, or a combination of the two, open and close jump rings by twisting the ends away from each other in opposite directions (pulling the ends straight away from each other will distort the ring).

**Stringing a jump ring** For a quick and simple dangle, open a jump ring wide and string a bead before closing (this works best with jump rings made of thin wire and beads with larger holes).

## SIMPLE LOOP
Use flat- or chain-nose pliers to form a 90° bend ¼–½" (6 mm–1.3 cm) from the end of your wire.

Grasp the short end of the wire with round-nose pliers {Step 1} and roll the end toward the bend in the wire until the end meets the bend {Step 2}, readjusting the pliers as needed.

Trim the wire tail if it extends past the bend in the wire. While still holding the loop in the pliers, adjust the wire below the bend as needed to restore the 90° angle.

{Step 1}

{Step 2}

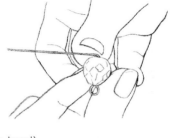

**Double-wrapped simple loop** Begin as if making a simple loop but bend the wire ½–1" (1.3–2.5 cm) from the end. After forming the loop, continue to wrap the wire around the pliers for a second time, creating a second loop on top of the first. Trim the wire at the point where it crosses the bend.

**Simple-loop link** Form a simple loop at one end of the wire and string a bead. To make the 90° bend close to the bead, snug the bead down to the first loop and use your fingers to fold the wire over the bead (or use flat- or chain-nose pliers to pull the end of the wire away from the bead). Form a simple loop to complete the link.

**Simple-loop dangle** Use a head pin to string 1 or more beads and form a simple loop.

**Attaching a simple loop** To attach a simple loop to a link of chain or other finding, open the loop like you would a jump ring.

## WRAPPED LOOP
Use flat- or chain-nose pliers to form a 90° bend ½–1" (1.3–2.5 cm) from the end of your wire. Make a simple loop but do not trim the tail. Grasp the loop with chain-nose pliers {Step 1}.

Use your fingers, or hold the end of the wire with a second pair of flat- or chain-nose pliers, and wrap the tail around the wire at the base of the loop {Step 2}. For tight wraps, think of pulling the wire away from the loop as you wrap. Trim the wire tail.

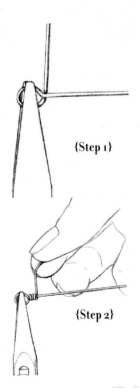

{Step 1}

{Step 2}

**Double-wrapped loop** Instead of trimming the wire tail, continue wrapping back up toward the loop on top of the previous wraps.

**Wrapped-loop link** Form a wrapped loop at one end of the wire and string a bead. Push the bead down to the first loop and grasp the wire just above the bead using the tip of your chain-nose pliers {Step 1}. Make the 90° bend {Step 2} and form a wrapped loop as before to complete the link.

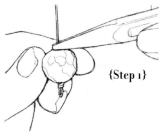

{Step 1}

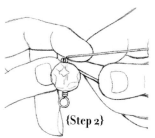

{Step 2}

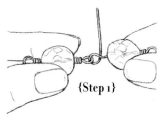

{Step 1}

**Connecting a wrapped-loop**
Make a basic wrapped loop, but before wrapping the tail at the base of the loop, string the chain link, clasp, link, or other finding {Step 1}.

Grasp the loop with tip of chain-nose pliers, holding the strung finding out of the way {Step 2}, and wrap the tail at the base of the loop as before.

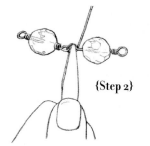

{Step 2}

**Wrapped-loop dangle** Use a head pin to string 1 or more beads and form a wrapped loop.

## BAILS

**Wrapped-loop bail** See p. 35 for detailed instructions on forming wrapped-loop bails. If you do not wish for the wire to extend down over the top of the bead, only make two to three wraps after forming the loop and trim the tail short.

**Trapped bead bail** Use 1½" (3.8 cm) of wire to string 1 bead. Position the bead so that it is about ½" (1.3 cm) from one end of the wire and bend both wires straight up.

Use both wire ends to string 1–3 assorted beads, trapping the short wire inside the beads; trim the short tail if it sticks out of the last beads strung. Use the remaining wire to form a simple loop (as shown here) or wrapped loop to complete the bail.

**Wrapped-loop link with bail** Use 1½" (3.8 cm) of wire to string 1 bead. Position the bead so that it is about ½" (1.3 cm) from one end of the wire and bend both wires straight up.

Wrap the short end around the long just above the bead and from the extra wire. String 1–3 assorted beads using the remaining wire and form a wrapped loop above the beads to complete the link/bail.

## KNOTTING

**Overhand knot** Make a loop with your stringing material by crossing the left over right. Pass the left end through the loop from the back so that is resembles a pretzel. Pull the thread tight.

**Square knot** Working with two cords (or threads), cross the right end over the left end and wrap it around the left cord as if making an overhand knot. Make an overhand knot by passing the left end over and under the right and pull the threads tight.

**Lark's head knot** Fold your stringing material in half and pass the fold through the finding's ring or loop. Pull the ends through the loop of the stringing materials created by the fold and pull.

**Stringing** Simply use a wire (beading or gauge) or a needle and thread to pick up beads and gather them into a strand.

## STITCHING
### Pass through vs pass back through

Pass through means to pass through a bead a second time, moving the wire or needle in the same direction as the first pass. To pass back through, move the wire or needle in the opposite direction that the beads were strung.

## CRIMPING

**Crimp tubes** Use beading wire to string 1 crimp tube, pass through a finding, and pass back through the tube, leaving a ¼–½" tail (6 mm–1.3 cm).

Make sure the wires do not cross inside the tube. Pinch the tube into a U shape, using the back notch of the crimping pliers {Step 1}.

Turn the pinched tube 90° and use the front notch of the crimping pliers to fold it into a cylinder {Step 2}.

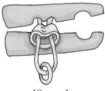

{Step 1}

{Step 2}

### Crimp beads

Repeat as for crimp tubes but instead of crimping with crimping pliers, flatten the bead using flat-nose pliers.

### Crimp covers

Hold the cover in the front notch of the crimping pliers, position it over a crimped crimp tube, and gently close to form a bead. For a perfectly round crimp cover, rotate the pliers around the cover just before you pinch the cover completely closed.

## The right crimp for the right wire

Check with the manufacturer for a complete list for pairing crimp tube sizes with wire sizes. Here are a few general guidelines recommended by the Soft Flex Company for the most commonly used sizes:

**1x1mm crimp tubes** can accommodate: 1 strand of .014 wire and 1 strand of .019 wire.

**2x2mm crimp tubes** can accommodate: 8 strands of .014 wire, 4 strands of .019 wire, and 1 strand of .024 wire.

**2x3mm crimp tubes** can accommodate: 8 strands of .014 wire, 4 strands of .019 wire, and 2 strands of .024 wire.

**3x4mm crimp tubes** can accommodate: 31 strands of .014 wire, 20 strands of .019 wire, and 10 strands of .024 wire.

# start shopping

## *materials*

**AD Adornments**
kathyd33@yahoo.com
www.adadornments.com

**Art & Soul Beads**
326 Spring St.
Jeffersonville, IN 47130
(812) 285-0000
www.artandsoulbeads.com

**Art Heaven**
PO Box 4870
Tubac, AZ 85646
support@artheaven.net
www.artheaven.net

**Artbeads.com**
11901 137th Ave. Ct. KPN
Gig Harbor, WA 98329
(866) 715-2323
www.artbeads.com

**Austin Gem and Bead**
PO Box 719
Chestertown, MD 21620
info@beadivine.com
www.austingemandbead.com

**Ayla's Originals**
1511 Sherman Ave.
Evanston, IL 60201
(847) 328-4040
www.aylasoriginals.com

**Bead Cache**
3307 S. College Ave.,
Unit 105
Ft. Collins, CO 80525
(970) 224-4322

**Bead Goes On, The**
PO Box 592
14 Church St.
Vineyard Haven, MA 02568
(866) 861-2323
www.beadgoeson.com

**Beadbury & We're**
**Stampin' Mad**
300/308 5th Ave. SE
Osseo, MN 55369
(763) 425-4520
www.beadbury.com

**Beadcats**
PO Box 2840
Wilsonville, OR 97070
(503) 625-2323
www.beadcats.com

**Beadin' Path, The**
15 Main St.
Freeport, ME 04032
(877) 92-BEADS
www.beadinpath.com

**Beads and Beyond**
25 102nd Ave. NE
Bellevue, WA 98004
(425) 462-8992

**Breckenridge Bead Gallery**
224 S. Main
Breckenridge, CO 80424
(970) 453-1964

**Beyond Beadery**
PO Box 460
Rollinsville, CO 80474
(800) 840-5548
www.beyondbeadery.com

**Bokamo Designs**
5609 W. 99th St.
Overland Park, KS 66207
(913) 648-4296
www.bokamodesigns.com

**Bonita Creations**
**& Gemstones**
(310) 490-0548
info@bonitacreations.com
www.bonitacreations.com

**Capture Scrapbooking**
**+ Paper Crafting**
838 W. Drake Rd., #105
Fort Collins, CO 80526
(970) 484-0595
www.shopcapture.com

**Dakota Stones**
7279 Washington Ave. S.
Edina, MN 55439
(866) 871-1990
www.dakotastones.com

**Denver Fabrics**
2777 W. Belleview Ave.
Littleton, CO 80123
(303) 730-2777
www.denverfabrics.com

**Desert Gems**
457 Wadsworth Blvd.
Lakewood, CO 80226
(303) 426-4411
www.desertgemsinc.com

**Dick Blick Art Materials**
PO Box 1267
Galesburg, IL 61402
(800) 828-4548
www.dickblick.com

**Family Glass**
(913) 231-1313
familyglass@familyglass.com
www.familyglass.com

**Fire Dragon Beads**
5095 Upper Elm St.
Atlanta, GA 30349
(770) 739-0057
www.firedragonbeads.com

**Fire Mountain Gems and Beads**
1 Fire Mountain Wy.
Grants Pass, OR 97526
(800) 423-2319
www.firemountaingems.com

**Funky Hannah's**
324 Main St.
Racine, WI 53403
(262) 634-6088
www.funkyhannahs.com

**FusionBeads.com**
13024 Stone Wy. N.
Seattle, WA 98133
(888) 781-3559
www.fusionbeads.com

**Galena Beads "serving**
**creativity"**
109 N. Main St.
Galena, IL 61036
(815) 777-4080
www.galenabeads.com

**Glass Garden Beads**
413 Division St. S.
Northfield, MN 55057
(507) 645-0301
www.glassgardenbeads.com

**Global Curiosity**
PO Box 7673
Princeton, NJ 08543
(877) 495-3872
www.rucurio.com

**Green Girl Studios**
PO Box 19389
Asheville, NC 28815
(828) 298-2263
www.greengirlstudios.com

**Hannah Grey Curiosities**
**& Drygoods**
PO Box 36187
San Jose, CA 95158
(408) 892-5726
www.hannahgrey.com

**Hands of the Hills**
(wholesale only)
3016 78th Ave. SE
Mercer Island, WA 98040
(206) 232-4588
www.hohbead.com

**Heather Wynn**
PO Box 6474
Gulf Breeze, FL 32563
heather@heatherwynn.com
www.heatherwynn.com

**Hobby Lobby**
www.hobbylobby.com

**Jess Imports**
(wholesale only)
110 Gough St., #203A
San Francisco, CA 94102
(415) 626-1433
www.jessimports.com

*Check your local bead shop or contact the companies below to obtain many of the materials used in this book. Remember that suppliers may have limited quantities, so don't hesitate to substitute the featured materials with your own favorite beads and findings. See pp. 140–142 for a resource guide to each chapter.*

**Jo-Ann Fabric and Craft**
(888) 739-4120
www.joann.com

**Knot Just Beads**
515 N. Glenview Ave.
Wauwatosa, WI 53213
(414) 771-8360
www.knotjustbeads.com

**Let It Bead**
821 Englewood Pkwy.
Englewood, CO 80110
(303) 788-1466

**Lillypilly Designs**
PO Box 270136
Louisville, CO 80027
(303) 543-8673
www.lillypillydesigns.com

**Luna's Beads & Glass**
PO Box 4691
416 E. Main St.
Frisco, CO 80443
(970) 668-8001
www.lunasbeads.com

**Marsha Neal Studio**
PO Box 1560
Hockessin, DE 19707
marsha@marshanealstudio.com
www.marshanealstudio.com

**Michaels**
(800) 642-4235
www.michaels.com

**Michele Goldstein**
PO Box 7294
Salem, OR 97303
meesh@michelegoldstein.com
www.michelegoldstein.com

**Mother Beads**
152 Legend Oaks Wy.
Summerville, SC 29485
renee@motherbeads.com
www.motherbeads.com

**Niki Passenier**
PO Box 1744
Albany, OR 97321
nikipassenier@gmail.com

**Nina Designs**
PO Box 8127
Emeryville, CA 94662
(800) 336-6462
www.ninadesigns.com

**Northern Colorado Stained Glass Supply**
PO Box 380
3000 N. Overland Trl.
Laporte, CO 80535
(970) 482-7655
www.ncstainedglass.com

**On the Surface**
PO Box 8026
Wilmette, IL 60091
info@onsurface.com
www.onsurface.com

**Ornamental Resources**
1427 Miner St.
Idaho Springs, CO 80452
(800) 876-6762
www.ornabead.com

**Ornamentea**
509 N. West St.
Raleigh, NC 27603
(919) 834-6260
www.ornamentea.com

**Orr's Trading Co.**
3422 S. Broadway
Englewood, CO 80110
(303) 722-6466
www.orrs.com

**Raven's Journey International**
PO Box 3099
Port Angeles, WA 98362
sales@theravenstore.com
www.theravenstore.com

**Rishashay**
PO Box 8271
Missoula, MT 59807
(800) 517-3311
www.rishashay.com

**Riverstone Bead Co.**
6131 Hemlock Ave.
Miller Beach, IN 46403
(219) 939-2050
www.riverstonebead.com

**RocknRocks**
111 Franklin St.
Clarksville, TN 37040
(931) 920-4055
www.rocknrocks.com

**Rocky Mountain Bead Trader**
2750 S. Broadway
Englewood, CO 80113
(303) 781-2657

**Shiana**
www.shiana.com

**Shrinky Dinks/K & B Innovations**
PO Box 223
North Lake, WI 53064
(800) 445-7448
www.shrinkydinks.com

**Singaraja Imports**
PO Box 4624
94 Main St.
Vineyard Haven, MA 02568
(800) 865-8856
www.singarajaimports.com

**Stone Mountain Colorado**
PO Box 1250
Walsenburg, CO 81089
(719) 738-3991

**Susan Lenart Kazmer**
23216 E. Echo Lake Rd.
Snohomish, WA 98296
(206) 910-8243
www.susanlenartkazmer.net

**Treasure Island**
1329 Lily Cache Ln.
Bolingbrook, IL 60490
(630) 759-2323
www.treasureislandbeads.net

**Two Hands Paperie**
803 Pearl St.
Boulder, CO 80302
(303) 444-0124
www.twohandspaperie.com

**Via Murano**
17654 Newhope St., Ste. A
Fountain Valley, CA 92708
(877) VIAMURANO
www.viamurano.com

**Vintaj Natural Brass Co.**
(wholesale only)
PO Box 246
Galena, IL 61036
info@vintaj.com
www.vintaj.com

**Whole Bead Shop, The**
PO Box 1100
Nevada City, CA 95959
(800) 292-2577
www.wholebeadshop.com

## magazines

**Cloth Paper Scissors**
clothpaperscissors.com
**Step by Step Beads**
stepbystepbeads.com
**Step by Step Wire Jewelry**
stepbystepwirejewelry.com
**Stringing**
stringingmagazine.com

## websites

interweave.com
beadingdaily.com

## bead shows

beadexpo.com
beadfest.com
wirejewelryfest.com

# project resources

*Check your local bead shop for the materials used in this book or contact the companies listed here (see pp. 138–139 for contact information). Many of the general crafting supplies such as fabric and scrapbooking materials can be found at local and chain craft stores. Below you will find references to many beads and findings that are not needed to create the featured pendants, charms, and clasps. Instead, they are shown attached to many samples and mentioned in the Stringing Suggestion sidebars. Unless otherwise noted, the materials used in the samples and projects are from the author's collection. Remember, many vintage beads and findings are limited in availability; if the companies don't have the exact beads shown in this book, they will most probably have something similar that will work just as well, so don't be afraid to mix it up.*

## pendants

### NOUVEAU RICHE RINGS P. 10

Gold-filled and sterling silver chain, natural brass bead caps and chain links, bead hoop, silver gauged wire, head pins, and Swarovski crystal rings, rounds, and bicones: FusionBeads.com. Gold-filled wire: Fire Mountain Gems and Beads. Bronze tapered ovals, gold-lined rondelles, labradorite faceted rounds, and jade teardrops: Luna's Beads & Glass. Etched shell donut: Lillypilly Designs. Amazonite teardrops and lemon quartz briolette: Fire Dragon Beads. Stamped silver long-and-short chain: AD Adornments. Antique rose fire-polished rounds: Raven's Journey International. Labradorite briolettes: Dakota Stones. Rutilated quartz rounds: Rocky Mountain Bead Trader.

### ETCH-A-BEAD P. 14

Black, clear, gold-rimmed gray, and gold-rimmed purple pendants: The Beadin' Path. Green and black gold-rimmed ovals: Glass Garden Beads. Swarovski crystal briolettes and bicones: FusionBeads.com. Dusty purple rondelles: The Bead Goes On. Smoky topaz squares and rondelles: Dakota Stones. Vintage Lucite rounds: Art & Soul Beads. Glass etching cream: Michaels.

### CLASSY COILS P. 16

Deer charm: Green Girl Studios. Silver wire, gunmetal craft wire, beading wire, jump rings, head pin, and Swarovski crystals: FusionBeads.com. Garnets: Riverstone Bead Co. Silver

bead frames and cone: Singaraja Imports. Gold-filled wire: Fire Mountain Gems and Beads. Pineapple quartz: Desert Gems. Charlottes and seed beads: Orr's Trading Co. Vintage Lucite rounds: Art & Soul Beads. Pyrite cubes: Ornamental Resources. Fire-polished rounds: Raven's Journey International.

### FANTASTIC PLASTIC P. 20

Shrinky Dinks Shrinkable Plastic: Shrinky Dinks/K & B Innovations Inc. Grafix Shrink Film: Jo-Ann Fabric and Craft. Amazonite rounds and fire-polished rounds: Let It Bead. Seed beads: Orr's Trading Co. Vintage Lucite rounds: Art & Soul Beads. Jump rings: FusionBeads.com.

### FLIRTY FRAMES P. 24

Thai silver rings: Shiana. Silver craft wire, sterling silver and gold-filled chain, sterling silver jump rings, and gold-filled head pins: FusionBeads.com. Aquamarine rondelles: Desert Gems. Labradorite teardrops and topaz rondelles: Dakota Stones. Brass frames and sterling silver 30x54mm frame: Art Heaven. Gold-filled and all other sterling silver frames: Singaraja Imports. Bird bead: Green Girl Studios. Daggers: Luna's Beads & Glass. Teardrops, pressed-glass leaves with simple loops, and fire-polished rounds: Raven's Journey International. Black leaves with wires, and antique brass jump rings, head pins, and chain: Ornamentea. Vintage—Lucite rounds: Art & Soul Beads. Gold-filled wire: Fire Mountain Gems and Beads. Pressed-glass flower: Bokamo Designs.

### IMPRESSIONABLE CLAY P. 28

Fimo polymer clay, stamps, and ink: Jo-Ann Fabric and Craft. Head pins, beading wire, assorted craft wire, and Swarovski crystals: FusionBeads. com. Cement, chain, and assorted jump rings: Ornamentea. Aquamarine and pineapple quartz: Desert Gems. Charlottes: Orr's Trading Co. Smoky topaz rondelles: Dakota Stones. Fire-polished rounds: Raven's Journey International. Bronze tapered ovals: Luna's Beads & Glass. Briolette and gold-filled wire: Fire Mountain Gems and Beads.

### Élan Lace (sidebar) P. 33

Silver jump rings, Swarovski crystals, chain, and wire: FusionBeads.com. Fire-polished rounds: Raven's Journey International. Charlottes: Orr's Trading Co. Triangle and other seed beads: Bead Cache. Aquamarine rondelles: Desert Gems.

### TOP IT OFF P. 34

Amber/white smooth briolette, and copper rounds: Luna's Beads & Glass. Jade 15x24mm faceted teardrop: Breckenridge Bead Gallery. Yellow turquoise 30x40mm briolette, chita 22x30mm briolette, and honey opal rounds: Dakota Stones. Cathedral beads and fire-polished rounds: Raven's Journey International. Crystal dagger: Northern Colorado Stained Glass Supply. Light green 7x18mm cubic zirconia teardrop, jump ring, and craft and sterling silver wire: FusionBeads.com. Light green and yellow 7x14mm cubic zirconia teardrops, smoky topaz 12x18mm

glass briolette, and gold-filled wire: Fire Mountain Gems and Beads. Amazonite teardrops and lemon quartz briolette: Fire Dragon Beads. Aventurine 16x28mm faceted teardrop and kyanite 6x24mm rough-cut dagger: Bonita Creations & Gemstones.

### PATCHWORK PANACHE P. 38

Eyelets, fabric, floral and abstract rubber stamps, ink, ribbon, embroidery thread, needles, and fusible web: Jo-Ann Fabric and Craft. Hole punch and eyelet setter: Two Hands Paperie. White/brown rondelles: Bokamo Designs. Rectangle jump ring: Ornamentea.

### IT'S IN THE CARDS P. 42

Bright brass frame, antique French reproduction playing cards, and brass solid and filigree wings: Hannah Grey Curiosities & Drygoods. Jump rings, Memory Frames, and Memory Glass: Ornamentea. Citrine rounds: Desert Gems. White/yellow faceted pressed-glass rondelles: Bokamo Designs. Smoky topaz faceted ron-delles: Dakota Stones. Rose/topaz fire-polished rounds and dusty rose pressed-glass rondelles: Raven's Journey International. Charlottes: Orr's Trading Co. Seed beads: Bead Cache. Brown striped vintage Lucite rounds: Art & Soul Beads.

### Locked in Time (sidebar) P. 45

French antique reproduction playing cards, bee charms, and cream-colored skeletonized leaves: Hannah Grey Curiosities & Drygoods. Antique watch parts, bird charm, jump rings, and "pocket watch" lockets: Ornamentea.

Hinged and 2-pane glass lockets: Jess Imports. Amazonite rounds: Let It Bead. Seed beads: Bead Cache. White pressed-glass flowers: Bokamo Designs. Mint green pressed-glass flowers: Raven's Journey International. Vintage Lucite rounds and rings: Art & Soul Beads. Yellow matte and striped blue glass rounds: The Bead Goes On. Micro glass balls: Luna's Beads & Glass.

### CABOCHON CRAZE P. 46
Fire-polished rounds, teardrops, bronze pressed-glass nuggets, and black/gold and green/silver buttons: Raven's Journey International. Handpainted Russian bead: Global Curiosity. Terrifically Tacky Tape double-sided craft tape: FusionBeads.com. Seed beads: Bead Cache. Charlottes: Orr's Trading Co. Vintage 1956 Olympic pin: Beads and Beyond. Dusty purple rondelles: The Bead Goes On. Labradorite rounds: Dakota Stones. Green/amber mottled rondelles, turquoise/black fire-polished rounds, and black/green mottled 3-sided rounds: Luna's Beads & Glass. Eye closures: Susan Lenart Kazmer. Bails: Bokamo Designs.

### WHIMSICAL & WEIGHTLESS P. 50
Gray and mint Vintage Lucite rounds: Art & Soul Beads. Moss green matte Vintage Lucite rounds: The Beadin' Path. Serpentine rondelles and lemon quartz rounds: Desert Gems. Fire-polished rounds pressed-glass nugget: Raven's Journey International. Engraved shells: Lillypilly Designs. Jasper rounds: RocknRocks.

### FRONT & CENTER P. 54
Cubic zirconia teardrop, gold-filled chain, Swarovski crystal bicones, brown craft wire, and sterling silver wire and head pins: FusionBeads .com. Box and bird clasps: Jess Imports. Extender toggle clasp: Niki Passenier. Nailhead coins: Stone Mountain Colorado. Smoky quartz: Dakota Stones. Thai silver toggle clasp, irregular rings, and charms: Shiana. Pressed-glass oval and kelly green

flower: The Beadin' Path. Antique copper chain, jump rings, and filigree: Ornamentea. Pale green marbled flowers: Bokamo Designs.

### THE MORE THE MERRIER P. 58
Mermaid charm: Green Girl Studios. Seed beads: Bead Cache. Jade teardrop and copper rounds and head pins: Luna's Beads & Glass. Lemon quartz briolette: Fire Dragon Beads. Engraved shell teardrop pendant: Lillypilly Designs. Swarovski crystal, brown craft wire, and sterling silver gauged wire and round chain: FusionBeads .com. Garnet rounds: Ornamental Resources. Brown swirls pendant: Marsha Neal Studio. Fine silver printed pendant: Bokamo Designs. Vintage Lucite rounds: The Beadin' Path. Pale green and bronze fire-polished rounds: Raven's Journey International. Cloudy gray fire-polished rounds: Let It Bead.

### Vintage to Vogue (sidebar) P. 63
Silver chain: AD Adornments. Pressed-glass flowers and rondelles: Raven's Journey International. Brooch converters: Fire Mountain Gems and Beads. Smoky topaz rondelles: Dakota Stones. Charlottes: Orr's Trading Co. Wire, Swarovski crystal rounds, and natural brass chain: FusionBeads.com. Seed beads: Luna's Beads & Glass.

### TINY TINS P. 64
Teal vintage Lucite rounds: Art & Soul Beads. Moss green vintage Lucite rounds: The Beadin' Path. Seed beads: Luna's Beads & Glass. Serpentine spacers: Rocky Mountain Bead Trader. Bone disc spacers: Ayla's Originals.

## charms

### CHARMING CAPS & CONES P. 70
Pressed-glass rondelles: Bokamo Designs. Silver and gold-filled head pins and all cones and bead caps: FusionBeads.com. Labradorite rounds and

smoky topaz rondelles: Dakota Stones. Antique brass head pins: Ornamentea. Spotted rounds: The Bead Goes On.

### SPLASH OF PATTERN P. 72
Charms: Small round gold and pointed oval Thai silver charms: Shiana. Jump rings and teardrop and round bezels: Ornamentea. Long tabular charms: Luna's Beads & Glass. Diamond charm: Jo-Ann Fabric and Craft. Other oval charms: Niki Passenier. 7 Gypsies rub-on: Capture Scrapbooking + Paper Crafting. Citrine rounds: Desert Gems. 2-hole coins: Raven's Journey International. Swarovski crystals: FusionBeads.com.

### SOFT & SWEET P. 74
Eyelets, fabric, and fusible web: Jo-Ann Fabric and Craft. Hole punch and eyelet setter: Two Hands Paperie. Fire-polished rounds: Bead Cache. Glass rondelles: The Bead Goes On.

### CHARMS MÉLANGE P. 76
Judi-Kins Diamond Glaze dimensional adhesive; antique watch parts; jump rings; The World's Tiniest Tarot Cards deck; bright brass heart, owl, peacock, heart, and bird charms; Amazing Glaze; strip of patterned copper; filigree pieces; antique watch parts; and antique brass and copper; round, teardrop, and rectangle bezel settings: Ornamentea. Round, winged, and teardrop pewter bezel settings: Green Girl Studios. Pointed-oval charms: Shiana. Diamond charms, stickers, and scrapbooking paper: Jo-Ann Fabric and Craft. Rose vintage Lucite rounds: The Beadin' Path. Green/red/white spotted rounds and dusty rose glass rondelles: The Bead Goes On. Silver and antique copper and brass small round charms and teardrop charm: AD Adornments. Seed beads and charlottes: Orr's Trading Co. Easy Cast Clear Casting Epoxy by Castin' Craft/Environmental Technology Inc.: Beadbury & We're Stampin' Mad and Dick Blick Art Materials. Amazonite rounds: Let It Bead. Pressed-glass

flowers: Bokamo Designs. Copper rounds: Luna's Beads & Glass. Aquamarine rounds: Treasure Island. Filigree wings and skull and retro star charms: Hannah Grey Drygoods & Curiosities. Silver 24mm square and 25mm round deep bezels: Beadbury & We're Stampin' Mad. Sterling silver bezels and links and cogged heishi washers: Susan Lenart Kazmer. Swarovski crystals, head pins, and craft wire: FusionBeads .com. Rutilated quartz: Rocky Mountain Bead Trader.

### BITS & PIECES P. 82
Swarovski crystals, wire, jump rings, and head pins: FusionBeads.com. Teardrop and gold round and square bead frames: Singaraja Imports. Thai silver detached chain links: Shiana. Fire-polished rounds: Raven's Journey International. Teal glass cubes: Let It Bead. Black cubes and hexagonal bead frames: Luna's Beads & Glass. Pressed-glass flowers and faceted pressed-glass rondelles: Bokamo Designs. Onyx ovals: Dakota Stones. Thai silver spacers: Hands of the Hills.

## clasps

### BEADED RING TOGGLES P. 86
Citrine rounds: Desert Gems. Wire, FireLine, Swarovski crystal bicones, head pins, and natural brass twigs: FusionBeads.com. Garnet rounds: Riverstone Bead Co. Labradorite and honey opal rounds: Dakota Stones. K.O. polyester thread: Beadcats. Fire-polished rounds: Raven's Journey International. Mother-of-pearl bead frame and amazonite rounds: Let It Bead. Vintage Lucite ring: The Beadin' Path. Similar wood bead frame: Artbeads.com. Filigree ring and rhodium-plated 3" (75 mm) head pin: Ornamentea.

### CHARMED CHAINS P. 90
Swarovski crystals, chain, prairie green 4mm fire-polished rounds, crimp tubes and beads, head pins, jump rings, natural brass charms,

# project resources

gold-filled 22-gauge dead-soft wire, sterling silver 24-gauge wire, sterling silver lobster clasp, and French rose fire-polished rounds: FusionBeads.com. Gold-filled 24-gauge wire: Fire Mountain Gems and Beads. Seed beads, amber mottled rondelles, nuggets, mottled green 4mm fire-polished rounds, tapered ovals, and black/green mottled 3-sided rounds: Luna's Beads & Glass. Amazonite rounds: Let It Bead. Garnets: Ornamental Resources. German gold lobster clasp: The Whole Bead Shop. Aquamarine rondelles: Desert Gems. Natural brass head pins, chain, bead caps, and lobster clasp: Vintaj Natural Brass Co. (wholesale only) or Galena Beads "serving creativity" (retail). Thai silver flower bead caps: Niki Passenier.

## LASSO LOOPS P. 94

Polymer round: Heather Wynn. Charlottes, size 8° seed beads, and glass rondelles: Orr's Trading Co. Size 11° seed beads and faceted garnets: Bead Cache. Vintage Lucite rounds: Art & Soul Beads. Oval vintage button: On the Surface. Wood rondelles: Ayla's Originals. C-Lon cord: Knot Just Beads. Fire-polished rounds: Raven's Journey International. Smoky topaz rondelles: Dakota Stones. Horse charm: Green Girl Studios. Pineapple quartz and serpentine rondelles: Desert Gems. Thai silver bead caps: Niki Passenier. Thai silver spacers: Hands of the Hills. Wood squares: Let It Bead. Green rutilated quartz: Rocky Mountain Bead Trader.

## BEADY HOOKS & EYES P. 98

Swarovski crystal bicones and rounds, gunmetal craft wire, filigree round, hammer, and bench block: FusionBeads.com. Silver and gold-filled wire: Fire Mountain Gems and Beads. White-lined clear drops: Bead Cache. Borosilicate rondelles: Family Glass.

Silver clasp hook: Susan Lenart Kazmer. Aquamarine rondelles, serpentine, and pineapple quartz: Desert Gems. Cream/brown pressed-glass rondelles: Bokamo Designs. Dusty purple rondelles: The Bead Goes On. Mustard/pink spotted lampworked rondelles: Mother Beads.

## Distress It (sidebar) P. 100

Novacan Black Patina (for lead solder): Northern Colorado Stained Glass Supply. Liver of sulfur: Fire Mountain Gems and Beads. Wood squares: Let It Bead. Citrine rounds: Desert Gems. Swarovski crystal rounds: FusionBeads.com. Round Thai silver toggle clasp with offset opening: Shiana. Other assorted clasps, hooks, and jump rings: Bead Cache, Fire Mountain Gems and Beads, Niki Passenier, Ornamentea, and FusionBeads.com.

## ORBITAL ENDINGS P. 104

Nailhead coins: Stone Mountain Colorado. Wire, Swarovski crystal bicones, crimp tubes, and push clasp: FusionBeads.com. Onyx ovals: Dakota Stones. Serpentine rondelles: Desert Gems. Fire-polished rounds: Raven's Journey International. Cogged heishi washers and antique bronze clasp hook: Susan Lenart Kazmer. Amazonite rounds: Let It Bead.

## WRAP IT UP P. 108

Box clasp: Jess imports. Charlottes: Orr's Trading Co. Swarovski crystals and silver and copper wire: FusionBeads.com. Gold-filled wire: Fire Mountain Gems and Beads. Thai silver and gold vermeil toggle clasps: Shiana. Garnet 4mm rounds: Riverstone Bead Co. Garnet 3mm rounds: Ornamental Resources. Hex-cut seed beads: Bead Cache. Pearls: Austin Gem and Bead. Textured gold chain: AD Adornments. Labradorite rounds: Dakota Stones. S-clasp: Niki Passenier.

## MILLEFIORI MESH P. 112

Silver-plated mesh box clasp: Knot Just Beads. All other mesh box clasps: Ornamentea. Teardrops and bronze fire-polished rounds: Raven's Journey International. Lentil beads and ruby, crystal celsian, and green luster pressed-glass flowers: FusionBeads.com. Springtime Simplicity seed beads: Bead Cache. Purple-lined clear and cranberry AB seed beads: Orr's Trading Co.

## *projects*

### FOREST FLOOR NECKLACE P. 118

Craft wire and natural brass head pins and chain: FusionBeads.com. Ball-end head pins: Rishashay. Moss green vintage Lucite rounds: The Beadin' Path. Pale mint green vintage Lucite rounds: Art & Soul Beads. Seed beads: Bead Cache. Mesh box clasp: Ornamentea. Pale green marbled flowers: Bokamo Designs.

### EYE CANDY BRACELET P. 120

Vintage Lucite round and ovals: The Beadin' Path. Lampworked rondelles: Michele Goldstein. Beading wire, crimp tubes, and crimp covers: FusionBeads.com. Silver wire: Fire Mountain Gems and Beads. Charlottes: Orr's Trading Co.

### SANTA FE NECKLACE P. 122

Sterling silver wire and bead caps: FusionBeads.com. Turquoise teardrops (small): Bokamo Designs. Mottled (large) teardrops: Raven's Journey International. Jump ring and donut bail: Bokamo Designs and Fire Mountain Gems and Beads. Beading foundation: Beyond Beadery. Cabochon: Stone Mountain Colorado. Clasp: Jess Imports. Seed beads and charlottes: Orr's Trading Co.

### FLORAL ROMANCE NECKLACE P. 124

Fimo polymer clay: Jo-Ann Fabric and Craft. Pineapple quartz: Desert Gems. Chain and charms: AD Adornments. Wire, head pins, and round gunmetal and silver jump rings: FusionBeads.com. Oval gunmetal jump rings: Ornamentea. Clasp: Nina Designs.

### A LOVE OF TRAVEL CHARM BRACELET P. 126

Blue/yellow striped and yellow matte glass rounds and Thai silver flower charms: The Bead Goes On. Marbled teal matte vintage Lucite rounds: Art & Soul Beads. Beading wire, silver jump rings, and crimp tubes: FusionBeads.com. Pewter 15x22mm teardrop bezel setting: Green Girl Studios. Lock-and-key toggle clasp, all other jump rings, all other bezel settings (including the antique brass 30mm round bezel and antique brass and copper 18x30mm teardrop bezels), antique watch parts, and brass bird, padlock heart, and peacock charms: Ornamentea. Pewter pinecone bead and skiers, giraffe, Coliseum, and leaning tower of Pisa charms: Beadbury & We're Stampin' Mad. Antique brass heart, Eiffel Tower, teardrop, and dragonfly charms: AD Adornments. Jack charm: Susan Lenart Kazmer. Thai silver 8x18mm pointed-oval charm: Shiana. Silver-plated 14x18mm diamond charm: Jo-Ann Fabric and Craft.

### LOVE BEES NECKLACE P. 128

Cranberry vintage Lucite rounds: The Beadin' Path. Gold charlottes: Orr's Trading Co. Nailhead coins: Stone Mountain Colorado. Bee charms: Hannah Grey Curiosities & Drygoods. Square link with circle bezel and clasp hook: Susan Lenart Kazmer. Heart charm and jump rings: Ornamentea. Vee-O Vogue textured ring: Via Murano. Fire-polished rounds: FusionBeads.com.

# index

# Create Beautiful Jewelry

## with these inspiring resources from Interweave

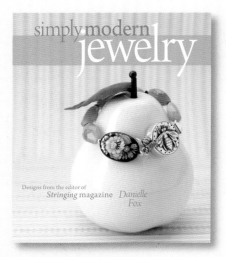

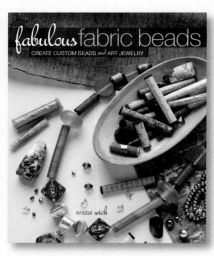

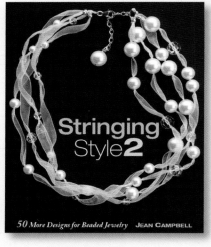

**Simply Modern Jewelry**
Designs from the editor of
*Stringing* magazine
DANIELLE FOX
ISBN 978-1-59668-048-7
$21.95

**Fabulous Fabric Beads**
Create Custom Beads
and Art Jewelry
KRISTAL WICK
ISBN 978-1-59668-077-7
$22.95

**Stringing Style 2**
50 More Designs for Beaded Jewelry
JEAN CAMPBELL
ISBN 978-1-59668-036-4
$18.95

## Are you Beading Daily?

Join BeadingDaily.com, an online community that shares your passion for beading. You'll get a free e-newsletter, free projects, a daily blog, project store, galleries, artist interviews, contests, tips and techniques, event updates, and more.

where life meets beading

**Sign up for Beading Daily
at beadingdaily.com**

## STRINGING MAGAZINE

The magazine for beaders who love stringing beads into bracelets, necklaces, earrings and more.

visit stringingmagazine.com

interweavebooks.com

# MANAGEMENT
# AND
# MACHIAVELLI